DOG
DAYS

D0188148

DOG DAYS

Life in Lockdown *with* Olive & Mabel

ANDREW COTTER

sourcebooks

Copyright © 2021 by Andrew Cotter
Cover and internal design © 2021 by Black & White Publishing Ltd
Cover design © Richard Budd Design
Front cover image © Susie Lowe
Internal design by Iolaire, Newtonmore
All photography unless otherwise credited © Andrew Cotter
Image on 326-327 © Iain Cameron

This publication is designed to provide accurate and authoritative information
in regard to the subject matter covered. It is sold with the understanding
that the publisher is not engaged in rendering legal, accounting, or other
professional service. If legal advice or other expert assistance is required,
the services of a competent professional person should be sought. —*From
a Declaration of Principles Jointly Adopted by a Committee of the American
Bar Association and a Committee of Publishers and Associations*

Published by Sourcebooks
P.O. Box 4410, Naperville, Illinois 60567-4410
(630) 961-3900
sourcebooks.com

Originally published in 2021 in Great Britain by Black & White Publishing Ltd.

Cataloging-in-Publication Data is on file with the Library of Congress.

Printed and bound in the United States of America.
VP 10 9 8 7 6 5 4 3 2 1

For Dexter. And optimists everywhere.

'But, Lord! how sad a sight it is to see the streets empty of people, and very few upon the Change. Jealous of every door that one sees shut up, lest it should be the plague; and about us two shops in three, if not more, generally shut up'

DIARY OF SAMUEL PEPYS,
Wednesday 16 August 1665

'Nothing open. Same walk again for the dogs. Watch a couple of episodes of The Golden Girls *on Channel 5'*

DIARY OF ANDREW COTTER,
Thursday 18 February 2021

INTRODUCTION

I have never kept a diary.

In fact, that's not strictly true. I do remember, at the age of seventeen, being informed that my services were no longer required in a relationship and deciding that I would thereafter commit to paper my profound thoughts each and every evening. I believe the plan was, that at some point in the future, this magnum opus might be discovered. Perhaps, decades later, a journalist would be browsing through a second-hand bookshop and chance upon it, reading slowly, mouth open, tears forming with every turn of the page as she fumbled for her phone to call her newspaper editor to clear some space for excerpts in the weekend culture section. And then…then people would understand and share my great pain, which few could possibly imagine or had ever experienced. I don't know where that diary is now – what I do know is that I put everything into it as I poured out my feelings and called from the depths of my ravaged soul, right up until the point where I abandoned it on day three.

Thankfully some people have a greater discipline in such matters and those who are more rigorous have given us invaluable chronicles of certain periods. One of the most celebrated works is, of course, the diary of Samuel Pepys, a man who liked to unwind after a hard day of seventeenth-century naval administration by jotting down all of the events that he had witnessed and often his innermost feelings. After initially putting pen to paper on the first day of 1660, his staying power in the endeavour – and an obvious penchant for sharing – meant that he rattled off more than one million words over the next decade or so.

He also had the fortune – bad for almost everyone, good for historians and future book sales – that he lived and wrote through some decidedly interesting times. Thus we have first-hand accounts of the Great Fire of London, the fear and suspicion as bubonic plague swept through the city and also the second instalment of a series of wars with the Dutch, which didn't go entirely according to plan for England.

The diary was significant for those major events but also because of the detail of the more mundane aspects of Pepys' life. The historical importance lies in the clear picture which he painted for us of late seventeenth-century London. Of course, now his diary would not really stand out as so many of us record our lives every day – more rarely on paper, but rather in photos, videos, podcasts and millions upon millions of posts on social media. Pepys today would not be scribbling away by the light of an oil lamp, but instead would be doing a heavily choreographed dance routine with his family on TikTok, while lip-syncing to Dua Lipa. Except he didn't have any offspring – only a long-suffering wife, as he appears to have been quite a one for the ladies – so it's more likely that he would have been posting work-out routines on Instagram or draping himself over the bonnet of a white Bentley in Dubai. He might even find time to make an animal video or two, although judging by his work he seems to have been very much more a cat person.

For the most part, the diary of Samuel Pepys is hardly a thriller, but in that lies its significance. He rambles on at great length about his health, frustrations with his work and deeply personal matters of his home life – all the seemingly trivial things that nevertheless resonate 350 years later. Give or take the odd skirmish with the Netherlands, we are still the same creatures – with the same strengths and weaknesses, the same insecurities and occasional need to be heard. It's just that our pen is different.

I suppose that it is one of the reasons why the videos I have made with Olive and Mabel have proved popular – because they have reflected something of the oddness of the time as well as perhaps providing some amusement when that has certainly not been the prevailing mood. I would imagine that they, rather than a diary, would be a more lasting record of the way we carried on with our lives which were so drastically altered.

Like Pepys we have been – and still are – enduring our own interesting times and have all been simply trying to make our way through it as best we can. I'm still entirely lacking the dedication required to keep a diary, but I did start taking note of some things that took place in 2020 and 2021, because of everything that was happening and because, frankly, the days seemed worthy of an account or two.

It's not just that the world at large was strange and difficult and that everybody had their lives so dramatically transformed, but that I was seeing it through an even more distorting prism as I continued to trot through life with two quite famous dogs. The concerns about employment, the feelings of isolation and the low moments were there for me as they were for millions of people, but thanks to Olive and Mabel, we were able to have experiences that would not otherwise have been possible. In unfortunate times we have been very lucky.

And yet one cannot help but become more philosophical when the world stops turning in its normal fashion. You think about your own lives and those of others. You ponder all the aspects of the way we exist as human beings – how we live and the things we do to help us on the journey.

Yes, the idea of a diary still makes me somewhat uncomfortable – with its subject matter personal, the musings and tone often self-regarding or confessional. And I'm also sure that for many a reliving of this period would be the last thing they would want to do, preferring to tear the pages from their memories and move swiftly on – but there might also be a dark humour to be found there and, who knows, once the years have passed and the distorting effect of nostalgia has kicked in, we may even like to remember at least some of these peculiar days.

So here are some recollections of things which occurred and the often very odd things we did to muddle our way through this strange time. A time when, at every turn, I've been so very glad that my own journey has been in the company of – and indeed shaped by – two beautiful, comical, optimistic and eternally hungry dogs. Both blissfully unaware of anything that is taking place in the wider world. Role models for us all.

OCTOBER 2020

Friday 9 October

It's a terrible thing to see a star struggling on stage, as I have witnessed tonight.

I suppose it happens to the best of them. I'm sure that once in a while Gielgud or Dame Maggie Smith would have momentary pause to try and remember a line or perhaps even have stumbled over a polystyrene rampart. But this evening the lead performer merely seemed distracted, wondering where she should be – at one point drifting aimlessly from one wing to another, before standing at the front of stage, mouth open and staring blankly into the lights. Thankfully this was when a member of the audience in the front row spotted an opportunity, rose from their seat, came forward and gently stroked her ears.

I'm not sure that anything we have experienced so far sums up the oddness of the Olive and Mabel thing quite like today – an appearance on stage at the Everyman Theatre in Cheltenham as part of the town's famous Literary Festival. I didn't know quite what to expect

– or rather wondered what the audience might have expected. One hundred had been allowed in under current guidelines and the tickets had disappeared fast. My concern was that half of them would get up and walk out after a few minutes, perhaps shouting obscenities while hurling their popcorn at us, to my shame and Olive's delight.

The surreal nature of the whole event had been evident from the moment we arrived at the hotel, where we were met by a very excited organiser and one or two people wearing headsets who were soon delegated to arrange a bowl of water for 'the headline act'.

The headline act had in the meantime decided that it was more in their interests to crash into the adjoining green room, where serious and seasoned authors were milling around and now having their serious and seasoned discourse interrupted by a dog or two appearing at their feet. On a few occasions it did look as if Olive was trying to sidle into the conversation with an amusing anecdote of her own, or more likely see if they might drop some crumbs her way – or even, such is her hopeful nature, that they would offer to fetch her a platter of assorted snacks from the buffet.

Then, after a couple of interviews, it was on to the theatre itself where we were escorted to a dressing room and Mabel padded nervously around as if trying to remember her lines, or where she was supposed to be during the opening number. I was more concerned that people would simply be bored and that, after the videos which had been enjoyed around the world, this live performance would be something of an anti-climax. Largely because there was no real performance planned – we were just supposed to sit on stage and talk.

But I needn't have worried. After I ambled out to a smattering of polite applause and took my seat with the moderator, friend and fellow broadcaster Jill Douglas, I settled into an armchair and we began our conversation.

Sparkling though our chat was, if we had carried on like that, I'm sure there would have been one or two raised eyebrows in the audience and perhaps even an audible muttering of 'Twenty quid for this bollocks?' but the more observant would have spotted the dog beds either side of my chair and I thought it best not to leave the crowd waiting too long. So, after a minute, we paused and I summoned the real stars from the wings where they were being held by my partner Caroline and they trotted happily onto the stage, to a noise that wouldn't have been heard in the theatre since Bobby Davro's seminal Hercule Poirot in *Death on the Nile* in 1987.*

What takes me aback is that this is the first time I have seen a mass reaction to these two dogs in real life. When you get the laughter and the pleasant messages

---

* *I'm pretty sure that such a production never took place. But it's late and I haven't got the energy to look up historic performances at the Everyman Theatre in Cheltenham.*

from thousands online, there is an acknowledgment but also a detachment. Here, the enjoyment is live and right in front of us. So when Olive rather loses her way – or realistically it is more that she is hunting for edibles – it is all part of the entertainment. As Mabel tenderly chews the stuffed rabbit beside me – possibly still hoping for some sort of prompt – Olive returns to her own bed, circles twice and collapses with a heavy sigh. All of which is enough for a round of applause.

We then show some of the videos on the big screen, I talk about the making of them, talk about the dogs, talk to the dogs. I do feel that the crowd deserves a little bit more after parting with their hard-earned cash, so every now and again I prod the dogs to life by stealing the rabbit, waving a bag of treats in front of their noses, or just lifting up an ear and folding it over to comic effect. But in truth it doesn't really matter what Olive and Mabel do, it is enough just that they are there. I think everyone involved was simply happy to escape from screens and enclosed lives and get into the real world, to have a night out and feel normal again – feel normal by purchasing a ticket to watch two dogs curled up in their beds.

Stranger still is to come as, once we have finished, we leave by the stage door to be greeted by dozens of audience members. Excited exclamations and chatter are followed by requests for photos. For a few minutes we are the Beatles – maybe not at the very height of the mania, but certainly getting close to the early days in Hamburg.

So I become Brian Epstein, gently easing myself out of the way and telling Olive and Mabel to sit properly as, one by one, the disciples move cautiously forward to say hello. Mabel looks rightly baffled and not a little concerned, Olive as if she has fully expected this attention and that it is entirely deserved. Eventually we have to pull ourselves away and walk down the street, dropping the dog beds every few paces, with just a few stragglers jogging after us and hoping for their own chat with the stars.

Back in the hotel I can reflect on it all. Nothing is normal at the moment, but this wanders ever deeper into abnormality by the day. Yet there's no denying it's great fun as well – to actually encounter some of the people who have enjoyed Olive and Mabel and to see their reactions upon meeting the dogs.

Meanwhile Lennon and McCartney are out for the night, twitching away and processing events, taking everything in their strides as they always do and happy to simply be with us.

Although now that I think about it, Mabel is probably Ringo.

Sunday 11 October

Michael Hutchence, Radiohead, Margaret Thatcher, Björk, Stephen Fry, Martin Scorsese, Lenny Kravitz and the Spice Girls.

While it does have the air of a guest list for nibbles and drinks at Richard Branson's house circa 1996, these are in fact just a few of the figures captured by the camera lens of Harry Borden. There is, apparently, more of his work hanging in the National Portrait Gallery than of any other photographer and the number and calibre of stars he has worked with is extraordinary. And to this list he can now add two dogs who were not entirely won over by his reputation.

Today was a photoshoot which had been organised by an American publication, *Outside* magazine, as they were keen to make Olive and Mabel two of their 'Outsiders of the Year'. Why not? I thought, in this new world which makes very little sense at all, and so the services of Mr Borden were enlisted. Whenever I have had reason to deal with any American organisation, I am baffled by the resources available to them. Thus a man who has had Morgan Freeman sit for him would now be trying to issue that literal instruction to a couple of Labradors.

In fact, it nearly didn't happen, with a frantic rush to get there, as beforehand I found myself doing what I used to refer to as 'my job', i.e. commentating on some sport. Since I have had only three days of such broadcasting in the last eight months, this couple of days – covering the PGA Championship golf – has been undeniably welcome but also unfamiliar. As we got underway there was a very strong possibility of me talking into the wrong end of the microphone, or enquiring of the producer, 'I see… And I just watch the pictures of the people hitting the ball and say some words? Well, let's give it a try.'

It was also less familiar since we weren't at the event itself – to be there I would have had to get into the strictly controlled 'bubble' at Wentworth Golf Club in Surrey by Friday afternoon. If that had been possible, I would have then been unable to leave until the event was over, awakening like Patrick McGoohan in *The Prisoner*, hemmed in by the fences and hedgerows of the exclusive estate and pursued by a giant white balloon if I tried to escape.

This was, indeed, the original plan, until I had to gently inform the editor that I was booked to appear on stage in Cheltenham with my dogs on Friday night. The fact that he barely raised an eyebrow shows that my reputation is now widely accepted.

As it happened, it all worked out well enough. Doing commentary off monitors from the BBC Sport base in Salford is far from ideal, but I was still able to race away at the end of the day's play to get to our appointment with Harry. It's unclear exactly how much experience he has had working with animals, but he appears to be learning as he goes along in this regard – discovering that while they might have less ego than some of his previous subjects, they also have remarkably short attention spans. Even shorter, perhaps, than the Spice

Girls. By the time I arrive there is only about half an hour of useable day remaining, but he quickly finds locations and light and ushers me into various poses and tries to do the same with Olive and Mabel, chatting away in the manner of the expert photographer and firing off shot after shot.

Caroline is thankfully on hand to both hold a reflector shield and break out the ever useful 'Ooh, here… what's THIS?' to get the dogs – and possibly me – to look in a certain direction. Although it only works briefly to attract their gaze and you have just a second or two to capture the moment before the dogs realise that the 'this' in question is a big fat nothing and they are being comprehensively lied to. The 'Ooh, whassis?' thereafter offers diminishing returns with their interest waning. Admittedly Olive grows weary of it well before Mabel who, thanks to a combination of goldfish memory and unerring trust, remains intrigued by the 'this' that Caroline promises she has, on at least five or six more occasions.

The shoot almost done, Harry spots that he might have a final opportunity – all three of us are asked to sit in the boot of my car and at one stage I find myself rolling around on the dog-hair-covered rug.

As we wrap up, our expert photographer seems pleased with what he has managed to get in the available time, but I am left wondering if he would have tried to get Margaret Thatcher to do this. On the way back home, Mabel asks Olive if she ever did find out what Caroline had hidden in her hand.

Wednesday 14 October

'Coming up, just after eight thirty, sports broadcaster Andrew Cotter is here – and more importantly he's bringing along his star dogs, Olive and Mabel...'

In this human-humbling fashion, our impending appearance on *BBC Breakfast* was announced this morning. Olive and Mabel are now seasoned pros on the circuit of light chat-based TV programmes, having featured on any number of channels at home and abroad during the spring and summer – that time we now refer to as 'all a bit mad'. Yet those appearances were remote – the dogs barely had to move from their beds or alongside me on the sofa and simply ate biscuits on cue to please Lorraine Kelly or Piers Morgan, while also pleasing themselves. Here we are out in the real world, meeting real people. Which somehow manages to feel enormously surreal at the same time.

We are, in fact, the first guests they have had in person on the programme for months, although we don't join them inside their familiar studio as the paperwork involved in getting a dog or two into the building was just too much. But thankfully it is dry outside and a weak sun even appears briefly – a minor miracle in a month where the country now resembles a giant sponge – and the effort they have put into the al fresco alternative is quite something, with an entire mobile studio created in the small garden across the square. Two bright red sofas are parked on the grass, with riggers dragging out lights and the attendant troops of people required to make television happen are suddenly there, milling around. Television is an unwieldy beast, yet still it appears that far more people than necessary are involved – very possibly claiming that they are vitally important, just to be allowed outside for a while. A producer and a couple of floor managers wearing headsets flit busily about as I produce a steady supply of biscuits for Olive and Mabel and we settle in to have a chat with presenter Louise Minchin.

The appearance is another chance to talk about the whole Olive and Mabel thing, but it is also loosely tied to publication of our book, *Olive, Mabel & Me*. I say 'our' book as if the dogs contributed in some way at all, but the collaboration was merely in them providing subject matter. And writing a book – actually *writing* it – signals only the start of the book-publishing experience. The clue is in the word 'publishing' as the only way to launch it successfully into the public domain is to let people know about it. And 'let people know about it' seems to be interpreted by anyone in the business as 'hitting people over the head with the availability of the book until they buy it out of weary submission'.

The vast majority of guests whom you see or hear on television or radio – especially at this time of year

– have a book to plug. Thus I have become one of those who will chat away on any topic, but both interviewer and interviewee are simply playing by the long-established rules of the game, until we arrive at the enquiry:

'And I hear you have a book out?'

At which point I am expected to look rather embarrassed and say, 'Goodness me, Louise – you've rather blindsided me with that question... Hahahaha... *naughty* of you...well, yes...yes, I do have a book out now that you mention it... Don't like to go on about it, but since you force my hand it's currently in stock at the following retailers...'

I suppose this is where I tend to come up short as a promoter. I don't like promotion – the concept of suggesting to everyone, no matter how subtly, that they should buy this thing because it's great. You see, it might not be great and, even if it were, I'm not too keen on saying such a thing. So instead I will probably end up muttering, 'Umm, yes, it's fine... I think,' and if you listen carefully enough, you will hear the gentle sobs of my publisher. I've never done praise well and self-praise even less so. I'm very wary of anybody who shouts too loudly about themselves – and you don't have to look too far to find a few of them these days.

But at the same time, this is pretty much my only employment this year. And besides, there are plenty of other people who have invested time and money into the project, so you have a responsibility to them – which is why we are here. And why Olive and Mabel are being pulled around from one interview to another, being fed comestibles to crunch into a microphone.

As it happens, Olive is entirely comfortable telling people how amazing she is, so, after a chat on BBC Radio 5 Live, she then bounds onto the TV set, greeting all and sundry in the Labrador way – either like old friends or like those who are on the brink of being befriended whether they want to be or not. You can see the effect it has on everybody as well – she is the person who is the life and soul of a party. An energy-bringer who works a room spreading joy even if they don't know, have never met, or simply can't remember the names of those whom they encounter. Her tail wags and body shakes, saying 'Hey, GREAT to see you fella... How are the kids?' 'Looking good there, Missy! Have you lost WEIGHT?'

The interview itself is over quickly. In the world of television, which operates on the belief that viewers have attention spans similar to that of your average spaniel, these things are always fleeting. It's mostly just an enjoyable chat about the dogs, with interludes of a couple of the videos, but it flies by as Olive falls asleep, having put all her energy into the initial meeting and Mabel occasionally looks for reassurance, but spends most of her time just staring into the distance.

Thankfully Louise, wonderful, professional, dog-loving person that she is, leaves plenty enough room at the end for us to deal with the most pressing issue affecting the world right now.

'Sooooo, tell us about this book of yours…'

'Louise, it is…a masterpiece,' I'm not quite bold enough to reply.

Thursday 15 October

There is a rare thrill in going into a bookshop to see something you have written sitting there. Up to this point there was still, in my head, the possibility of it all being an elaborate scam with the phone number of 'the publisher' no longer recognised and an investigative trip to their offices revealing an empty room with just an old folding-chair and a broken printer. But there it is – the jumble of words chosen and put into some sort of order over the last few months now existing as an actual book, with actual people browsing nearby. How satisfying that those actual people might have an actual desire to pick it up and actually take it home with them. I mean, nobody is when I am in there, standing conspicuously with the dogs beside the book, but if I hang around long enough who knows, I might see it happen. I even try picking it up now and again, leafing through the pages while making appreciative noises, or chuckling 'Ha, great stuff…' in the hope of piquing the interest of passers-by. But at the moment it seems rather overshadowed by the enormous piles of celebrity biographies which crowd around it. So I continue to stand for some time, signing those available copies whether anybody has asked me to or not and hoping that the sight of Olive and Mabel will soon result in an orderly queue of excited fans.

After about ten minutes of loitering, I quietly put my pen back in my pocket and slip away unnoticed. But, on the way out, take a moment to place copies of our book on top of *Once Upon a Tyne* by Ant and Dec.

Tuesday 20 October

In London today for an appearance on the Chris Evans Breakfast Show on Virgin Radio and I have to dig deep into my memory to remember the last time I visited the capital. It was certainly before the world changed. I'm not sure what I was expecting now – perhaps some dystopian, post-apocalyptic cityscape, where the only signs of human life are grubby urchins peering out from abandoned Costa coffees. In fact, it all seems quite pleasant, with everything still humming along – just London at a slower pace and with the volume turned down two or three notches. I notice it most of all as we walk across London Bridge, heading to the south side of the river at around eight in the morning. Where usually we would be struggling against a tide of commuters, all moving from London Bridge station to the City, now just a dozen or so people are there – each one of us doing the weaving two-metre waltz, the sway of personal space avoidance. Near enough impossible to perform successfully with a couple of dogs on leads.

But negotiate it we have to, because their company is most certainly requested here. Even on radio where the famous snouts and comical expressions can't actually be seen, the good folk of Virgin do still want to have Olive and Mabel in the studio and all necessary preparations have been made and paperwork completed. Although, when we arrive at the front desk, lengthy phone discussions still have to be undertaken as this is clearly not a regular occurrence and there remains some scepticism.

'Are they assistance dogs?' I'm asked, which does make me wonder how much help they think I need to have two on standby. Mabel answers in her own way, by beginning a particularly violent scratching session, which sends hundreds of little blonde hairs into the air, where they catch the sunlight coming in through the glass windows in a curiously hypnotic if somewhat unhygienic display.

'Not as such,' I reply as, behind me, the fur continues to drift down.

As much to be rid of us as anything else, we are finally permitted deeper into the building. And also higher – the studios are on the seventeenth floor, offering a grand view of the capital and a panorama which has been utterly transformed in the last twenty years. Not least thanks to the stretched glass pyramid of the Shard, which looms over us immediately next door as the tallest building in the land. But it is only the loudest of all the showy structures in this new skyline. How small by comparison St Paul's Cathedral now looks – built in its current guise after the Great Fire of London, it was once the giant itself, looking down on the rest of London for two and half centuries. But there it sits across the grey Thames with a quieter, more tasteful grandeur – a tether to the past, with all around it new buildings rising, crowding in, shouting for attention.

The height of our own building means that Olive has to do battle with both shiny floors and an elevator but she copes admirably. Far better than at the hotel last night where she had put the brakes on and point-blank refused to move once we left carpet and hit polished floor. Thankfully in her desperation to escape this private hell, she leapt onto one of the luggage trolleys and we were able to wheel her, like a mid-sized suitcase, to the lifts. What's more, she seemed to enjoy the process, moving along in stately fashion past the hotel manager, who forced a tolerant smile.

Here in the Virgin tower, no such nonsense is required (although she does hug the wall just to be on the safe side) and we are soon in the studio – granted an audience with the king. Chris Evans is at his enormous presentation desk with smaller tables, which are beyond a virus leap apart, for sports presenter Vassos and for me.

Breakfast radio presenters are a unique breed. They have extraordinary verve and, on-air at least, are always full of good cheer – thumb-up emojis in human form. Perhaps the most celebrated of all of them, Chris is one of those people who just has enormous energy, rivalling both Olive and Mabel for early morning enthusiasm, the major distinction being that he also has a fierce intellect – a mind which buzzes around at a frantic pace and therefore offers topics and questions which head off in any number of tangents.

You can easily see why Chris stands out, even in a very crowded field, and why he has done all that he has in radio and television. For the same reason that, earlier in his career, he could walk straight out of his studio and onto the front page of the tabloids, courtesy of enormous celebrity-filled benders. He would test the patience of employers, but still they wanted him back. Rules were changed and contracts altered for him and he was generally allowed to wander from the straight and narrow. Probably because he never delivered the straight and narrow on-air. And viewers and listeners kept tuning in.

But more than that, he just has something – that indefinable thing which great entertainers have. Something that you can't necessarily learn but which he is certainly able to switch on. And so it is here – quieter and more thoughtful while the music plays, the song ends, the microphone is faded up and the performance begins. Once more there is never anything bland or formulaic in what he offers, managing even to make a chat with a bloke about a couple of dogs sound interesting. Mabel doesn't even pretend that she is keeping up with the conversation, but does continue to scratch and deposits a reasonable amount of her tresses on the carpet. Olive stares at a packet of digestives on the desk brought in by the producer, either plotting her next move or hoping that she can make it fall by sheer force of will.

It is all very enjoyable, but eventually our time is up and we leave the studio with the clockwork-Chris still whirring away – onto some other segment and still holding court. His energy chases us down the corridor and fades only as the lift door closes. As we descend, Olive spreads herself wide and low, bracing for impact.

There is, though, still more to be achieved in London Town today. We had been asked a few months before if we would like to be featured on ABC's breakfast TV programme in America – another slightly absurd reminder of the transatlantic appeal of Olive and Mabel. But we have time to kill beforehand, so wander for a while through the city, taking in the sights and smells and sounds. It might be my imagination but it seems a curiously stress-free version of London – less traffic, far fewer people. And those who are here perhaps not quite so quick to temper over trivial matters, with all realising there is something greater to concern us. It is, however, still busy enough and yet Olive and Mabel – two dogs who are experiencing a metropolis for the first time – pad happily around, occasionally taken aback by a double-decker, but otherwise content to wander and sniff and browse and briefly attempt to stroll into the Apple Store on Regent Street.

An hour or two thus passed, we finish up the day heading to Richmond Park to meet our American TV crew for the recording, which will be broadcast at some indeterminate point in the future. And in a corner of this vast park, looking at its autumn best, we chat to reporter Maggie Rulli, who is thoroughly nice, but beyond that possesses the particular American joie de vivre which is a level up even from breakfast radio presenters and sufficient to make Labradors look curmudgeonly by comparison.

As another fellow dog lover, she has brought both treats and toys for Olive and Mabel, who we subsequently bribe for cooperation throughout the conversation. Then we set up a closing shot where I commentate as Maggie leaps about, throwing tug ropes for the dogs who look initially somewhat startled by this over-energetic human, but eventually play their part well.

With further biscuits being administered, we wrap it up – Olive and Mabel deciding that they have greatly enjoyed their trip to London. And what's more that they like American television and their food allowances very much. Very much indeed.

Monday 26 October

News arrives today that Olive and Mabel have been booked to appear at the London Palladium. Finally... I was starting to wonder when our talent for doing very little would be recognised.

Not for the first occasion, I reflect that these are indeed the most curious of days. But I am sent a photo by the organiser and there it is – on a billboard above the stage door of perhaps the most famous theatre in the West End, one human and two canine faces stare out. This is the venue of Royal Variety performances and 'Sunday Night at The London Palladium'. Any number of legendary acts have performed there, from Frank Sinatra, Bob Hope and the Beatles to the Rolling Stones, Elton John and the Krankies. Again, I ask myself the question, 'What are we expected to do?' as I am all too aware that Mabel's favourite routine of padding around and looking moderately anxious isn't going to keep the audience enthralled for long.

I spend much of tonight attempting to teach an older and younger dog new tricks, with repeated attempts to get Olive and Mabel to balance a biscuit on their nose before eating it. But it only ends in disappointment for me and a very fondly remembered evening for the dogs.

Saturday 31 October

Once more today I am reminded of what I was, and suppose still am, as sports broadcasting slowly but surely filters back into my life. I am required to commentate on Wales versus Scotland in the Six Nations rugby tournament, with further progress being made in that we are covering the event on site.

It feels significant for that reason and also because

this is the fixture which had effectively started everything Olive and Mabel-related. The one whose postponement back in March had tipped me over the edge and forced me out into the garden to commentate on the dogs eating. This game has a lot to answer for.

Yet any ideas that we have somehow completed the circle and normality has returned are fanciful in the extreme. The stadium for this rescheduled encounter is Parc y Scarlets in Llanelli, a much smaller affair than the original venue, the Principality Stadium in Cardiff, which is still out of action for sport, having being turned into an emergency Covid hospital. The size of the ground has little meaning though since there are, of course, no spectators – which always makes for a decidedly odd atmosphere. Here is a match in the Six Nations and you know very well that millions are watching on TV, but in the ground itself it feels like a training session. It also means that you can quite easily hear the players during the game. Usually drowned out by the crowd, they run around swearing copiously and I spend a good deal of the afternoon apologising for the language. It is also unsettling because the only other voices you can hear, punctuated by the occasional cry of 'Let's fucking go, boys', are those of the commentators – our more family-friendly words echoing around the empty stands. Players can probably hear us, and the coaching staff in the seats right in front of us most certainly can. In a match of deeply unimpressive quality, I make sure to describe every-body in glowing terms.

This, though, has also been a day when my twin occupations of life have clashed. I am mildly distracted before and after the game as I have been thinking about an Olive and Mabel Halloween video and, for fairly obvious reasons, it has to go out tonight. Throughout the whole journey back up the road I'm contemplating how it might work and by the time I make it home, mat-ters are fairly pressing.

Indeed, the reviews are barely in for the dogs' impro-vised 'Welcome Back' dance routine which greets me (3 out of 5 stars, 'Energetic, but lacking structure and form') before I herd them into position and explain to them the premise. Olive asks what her motivation is and so I rattle a Tupperware box full of chicken-flavoured treats, which seems to get her into character fairly effec-tively. Just like dear Judi Dench, I think.

As is always the way with these videos, the difficulty is in trying to get the dogs to enact what you have planned in your head. Caroline interrupts one of about fourteen subsequent takes to wonder aloud just what on earth I am doing. Since I am, at that precise moment, asking Olive why she has come dressed as a vicar and Mabel a nudist I can't immediately think of a suitable response.

NOVEMBER 2020

Sunday 8 November

I'm writing this while sailing on a late-night ferry across to Belfast. Heading to Northern Ireland on a very important mission to try and not humiliate myself.

I've been invited to make an appearance on *Celebrity Mastermind* – granted, in two key areas the programme title may well be in breach of the 1968 Trade Descriptions Act, but the chance to sit in the famous black chair on the UK's longest-running television quiz is still exciting.

The first thing you have to do, of course, is choose a specialist subject. Then largely bluff your way through to give the convincing impression that you are a leading authority in the field. I didn't want to select a sporting subject because it would put me in a no-win situation: get a few wrong and your credibility as a supposed expert is diminished. Stroll through them and your position is cemented as nothing but a sad sports geek – sport is your thing and all you know. You live and breathe sport. You are, forever more, Sporty MacSportsen. Instead, you hope to appear both scholarly and profound by your choice of a weightier topic, but then there is also danger in that, as you run the risk of being viewed as a colossal prick. Therefore I abandoned my brushing up (via Wikipedia) of the life of philosopher John Stuart Mill and went instead for the children's programmes of Oliver Postgate and Peter Firmin, creators of masterpieces such as *Bagpuss* and *The Clangers*.

The subject was supposed to be based more on the biography of Postgate himself, but a couple of weeks before filming I was informed by the production company that the questions would instead focus on the details of the actual episodes of the various programmes. Thus, while everyone else is spending their pandemic hours enjoying the latest great dramas or comedies on HBO or Netflix, I have been binge-watching DVD box sets of *Ivor the Engine*.

Sadly, the genuine celebrities aren't making the trip. I'm under no illusion that it is because of Olive and Mabel that I have been invited, rather than my seminal work in the field of sports broadcasting, so it's a real shame that they couldn't come, as was the original plan. I even had an idea that I could film a sketch where they were both contestants on *Mastermind* – Olive breezing through several questions about food, Mabel remaining firmly on zero as she was asked about particle physics or the Wars of the Diadochi. Discussions were had with the producers who initially were very taken with the idea and it did reach a fairly advanced stage – certainly in my head, at least, where I was contemplating how to get either dog to remain seated as the questions came in – but it was eventually turned down as the executive producer felt it might lead to many other such requests to abuse the famous black chair. And, what's more, the necessary upholstery cleaning after Mabel's turn would have put the programme markedly over budget.

So this is an entirely solo excursion and, since I wasn't keen on taking a plane at this delicate point in pandemic proceedings, here I am on an enormous white ferry, ploughing across the Irish Sea.

The vehicle deck is crammed nose to tail with lorries and mine is the only car on the entire ship, hemmed in by those involved in the transport of goods and materials and assorted stuff we've bought online – everything required to keep the country going. I do have a letter giving me permission to travel but it doesn't seem necessary. At the head of the queue to get on board there had been a couple of police cars and a van at a makeshift checkpoint, but they appeared to be chatting among themselves and happy enough to wave everybody through. I certainly didn't want interrogation to go any deeper, forcing me to justify my appearance on a TV quiz as essential work, claiming that it is absolutely vital for the morale of the nation that they see me furrowing my brow and trying to answer a few questions on *Noggin the Nog*.

No sooner have the multitude of truck drivers left the vehicle deck than they disappear into a lounge reserved solely for them. Behind the door it all sounds fairly lively in their haven of truck-based revelry, to which you are only admitted if you can give the secret sign – perhaps pulling down on an imaginary horn while making a honking noise. So I am left on my own, wandering round this modern *Marie Celeste*.

It doesn't seem that it might be the healthiest thing to be indoors anyway, so I move outside and climb to the upper deck, putting on all the warm clothing I have brought with me and now sit, running through the names of the cast of *Bagpuss* or, occasionally, to get away from the funnel and the bass throb of the engine, head over to lean on the rail and look out into the darkness.

On a cloud-filled night, almost everything beyond the ship is black and empty. With the sole light provided by the ferry itself and nothing at all to look at out there, I only know we're moving forward by the feel of the wind, or in watching the spray thrown out by the bow as it cuts through the rolling sea.

So I content myself to think about how fortunate I am to be here, to be out in the open. I let a fine rain blow across me and drink deep, free breaths of the salt air and I wonder about everybody in this world. I wonder where they might be or what they might be doing – all living our strange lives, every one of us sailing through the dark under a starless sky.

Monday 9 November

I may be without dogs, but with each rare trip I have been allowed to make it is a sort of liberation. And that's how it is here, simply to be able to get to Belfast – to have that change of scenery. Or it would be if the scenery were not quite so uncomfortably odd. Northern Ireland is in one of the highest levels of lockdown so, unlike the mainland (for the moment), nearly everything here is closed and the streets are quiet – only a few people to be seen, scampering through the rain which comes in on a hard wind off Belfast Lough. The hotel we're staying at is modern and luxurious and grand in scale but, like the ferry or the city itself, almost entirely devoid of life. Just two members of staff seem to be filling all the roles, as if in a small bed and breakfast run by a married couple. The same faces pop up behind reception, at the bar, in the restaurant, running here and there for the only guests – the contestants from the four or five *Celebrity Mastermind* shows which are being filmed today.

It creates a strange environment, wandering round an otherwise empty building, and in my head I am in an eerie work of science fiction where I'm one of only a few humans remaining…taken by surprise when occasionally rounding a corner to bump into somebody who looks equally shocked for a moment, before we solemnly agree that it's our responsibility to repopulate the earth. Although, in reality, that look of mine actually gives way to one of wondering just who they might be and if they are perhaps the person who checked me into reception a couple of minutes ago. More often we simply give an insider 'celebrity nod' to each other just in case, even if we haven't got the faintest clue and could do with a guidebook entitled *Low-level Celebrities of Western Europe – markings and identifying features*. Indeed, I spend much of my time explaining my presence, introducing myself as a sports broadcaster to polite feigned recognition, before backing it up with 'I do the Olive and Mabel dog stuff', which elicits genuine exclamations of approval. Hence a first encounter with writer and broadcaster Grace Dent, when a bonding over common Labrador ownership and love is possible. But, perhaps most exciting of all, I chat briefly to Neil Hannon, musical genius of the Divine Comedy, who expresses his affection for the Olive and Mabel videos.

Very soon this eclectic crew, a group unified only by a common denominator of minor public awareness, is back in school. We are all shown to carefully distanced chairs, arranged in neat rows, facing the front where we are to be briefed by the producers. The briefing doesn't really amount to much more than reminding us not to swear and letting us know when we can collect our outfits for the recording. I had winced when asked by the representative of the wardrobe department for my clothes to be taken away for pressing, as I handed over jeans and a jumper in a plastic bag. By contrast Hannon in particular is exquisitely turned out in a cream-coloured suit, but in a way that only actors or musicians are enti-tled to be. I feel that if I had tried something similar, the reaction would be as if I appeared wearing a monocle or a velvet cape.

As we prepare to leave for the studio, there is one final piece of upbeat and optimistic advice from the producer.

'If you can't think of the answer, then you know what to do? Have a guess – you never know, it might be right!'

This doesn't seem to me to be the wisest counsel as it only opens you up to potential ridicule and it is far more likely *not* to be right. Besides, my alternative plan of closing my eyes, grimacing and making high-pitched exasperated noises, before shaking my head, smiling ruefully and saying 'Pass' can suggest that, well…quite clearly I knew the answer but simply misplaced it under the pressure. Indeed, this effect can be augmented when the correct answers to the passes are given afterwards, by nodding sagely and muttering, 'Yes, yes…the Dutch East Indies…of *course* it is.'

However, by the time of recording, my brain is so befuddled that I forget to do this. In fact, it appears that I have forgotten how to walk when making my way to the chair and then, once we get going, fundamental words of the English language also escape me. Despite having strolled through the specialist subject round – and in the process shown myself in the unflattering light of being a middle-aged man with a firm grasp of children's television – the general knowledge round hits back. I would like to pretend that this is because the questions are incredibly difficult. Sadly I can't because it's not true. The producers know all too well that fame does not necessarily equal intelligence and, possibly for fear of getting an angry call from an agent after their client somehow scores negative points, they turn down the difficulty settings of this version of the game by a few levels: from expert...to hard...to standard...to easy...to bullmastiff...to celebrity.

No, the problem is more that under the pressure of the lights and the ticking clock and the gaze of the presenter John Humphreys, you begin to doubt yourself. Or worse, you simply draw an enormous blank. Thus I manage to mislay the word 'panini' for a toasted Italian sandwich and a gentle question about 'the metallic chemical element which has the shortest name of all the elements in the periodic table', brings nothing more than static in my brain with occasional interludes of circus music. I suddenly realise what it is like to live as Mabel, and, what's more, Humphreys is now me trying to get Mabel to understand simple instructions. So I cock my head slightly and stare, but the question might as well have been 'Which metal starts with the letter "t" and rhymes with "bin"?' and I would still have struggled.

A couple of wrong answers later and, with the only thing announcing itself in my memory being those perky words, 'Have a guess – you never know!' I do just that. Trying to think of an author who would fit the time reference in one question I go deep into speculation mode. 'Evelyn Waugh?' I suggest, despite being almost certain that it is not in any way correct. Humphreys' generous response to this is to actually laugh out loud, as if inviting everyone else to share in how silly I've been. Even with the clock ticking away, I make a mental note to find that producer afterwards.

Eventually the torture is brought to a merciful end. And with farewells said to celebrities and mere mortals alike, it's time to race to catch the last ferry of the day, which provides a repeat of the outward journey – the upper deck left entirely to myself while all sorts of high jinks and super-spreading goes on in the truckers' lounge below.

When reaching port again, despite my being parked at the bow of the ship, lorry after lorry is allowed to file out first, most of whom I know will be heading in the same direction on the long road out to reach the motorway. I smile as endearingly and plaintively as I can to the deck operator, but all to no effect, and I come to the obvious conclusion that this is an enormous conspiracy against me – one probably planned in that truckers' lounge and that's what they were laughing about. I am simply paying the price for not properly delivering the secret sign.

So I steel myself, preparing for an hour or so in a

slow-moving convoy of Eddie Stobart and friends. Yet I will gladly accept it since they all have a job to do and I am more than grateful for the experience which I have been allowed to have: given the very brief permission to be free, to do and see something different. To escape. That is more than enough compensation.

Well, that and a crystal *Mastermind* trophy, which sits twinkling on the passenger seat beside me.

God bless *The Clangers*.

Tuesday 10 November

It was nice while it lasted.

The whole of the country is now heading into a tighter level of controls and the wailing and gnashing of teeth can be heard up and down the land at the news that Olive and Mabel's appearance at the Palladium has been cancelled. For about two weeks we had been working through our routine – which had developed and evolved over time with numerous rehearsals and subsequent fine-tuning, tweaks and rewrites – eventually settling into one where I would sit in a chair with Olive and Mabel beside me, very probably asleep.

Tickets had, remarkably, been selling well and it is an enormous disappointment that our stagecraft and complex choreography is now not going to be seen. However, for the past week it has felt inevitable with the worsening situation and so it is no real surprise. And we are firmly aware of its lack of importance in the grand scheme of things. Or at least, I am. The awareness levels of the dogs remain low.

Yet as one opportunity disappears, others might be on the horizon with four different production companies now pitching four very different Olive and Mabel ideas to television channels. Since my branch of broadcasting doesn't often involve a commissioning process, it is left to others who have been heavily involved in this business for many years to explain to me the way it works. These production companies will come up with an idea for a programme and a format, then spend weeks drawing up the pitch, before presenting it to commissioning editors at a carefully selected channel within the dozens of available networks. The commissioning editors then weigh up all the factors and decide to go with something else.

Thus it becomes clear that the greatest requirement in getting a television series commissioned is a sense of patience and a realistic possession of low expectations, which is where I have always excelled. But in truth, a television series is not something that is high on my list of priorities. Mostly because I understand how time-consuming it can be to make programmes and I certainly know how difficult it can be to work with the dogs. Indeed, for some of the Olive and Mabel sketches it involves a few days' effort to come up with ninety seconds of screen-time. And, what's more, with every bit of filming that is required, I feel that I am asking a bit too much of them, even if they are quite happy to enjoy another take and one more snack.

So, it may well be that the grandest heights that Olive and Mabel will reach is on their very own YouTube channel, although at least there we are entirely in control. Olive and Mabel, operating as a small independent production company, present ideas to me and I – as the commissioning editor – make all the right noises about how well they've done, let them scamper out into the garden full of hope, before throwing their idea in the bin and deciding to do something entirely different.

Thursday 12 November

Nothing is normal but some things are more abnormal than others.

Once more there is sport to commentate on and for the smallest morsel of that I am very grateful, but if any event highlights the oddity of what we are doing now it is the Masters golf tournament. Not the actual event – although that in itself is strange, with the famous spring hues of Augusta replaced by autumn leaves – more so the way we have to work.

Peter Alliss, not far short of ninety years old, is the doyen of golf broadcasting and one of the few remaining great voices of British TV sport. But he can't be with us in person as he's currently in isolation because of his grand age; instead he has to join via a satellite feed from his home. And naturally the rest of us are currently unable to travel to the United States, so we are in the BBC studios. Augusta, therefore, has become a combination of Salford and (on a slight delay) Surrey. We commentate from a room which has been requisitioned for our needs and is officially called 'The Top Gear Room' as it is mostly used for production meetings for that programme. So, on one monitor we have the live action taking place in Augusta, on another Peter sitting in his dining room and we commentate with a cardboard cut-out of *Top Gear* favourite 'The Stig' watching over us all.

It is unquestionably odd, but strangely reassuring that we are able to come together and catch up – to find out what each of us has been doing to make our own way through these strange and testing months. To see other people in the flesh is such a simple thing, but means a great deal and offers a reassurance that there will be something else to return to on the other side of all this. Even if a lot of those people do now bark at me as I walk by.

Monday 16 November

I notice with some concern that for a few days now I have been wracked by a cough. It is one of those that emanates from deep within – somewhere around the knees – and it won't depart. I have, though, taken and passed any number of Covid tests, my temperature is steady as she goes at 36 degrees and my senses of taste and smell remain resolutely intact. For assistance in the ongoing symptomatic examinations, I am grateful to Mabel and the cloud of general damp dog aroma which tends to follow her around. So I remind myself that there are still coughs and colds out there which have nothing to do with the great menace.

Meanwhile, Twitter followers in America are letting me know that they feel rather sorry for Olive. For what, I'm not initially certain since she has had an enormously enjoyable day at the beach and has also just been given a small piece of banana.

After investigation I discover that the reason for the incoming pity is that a new edition of *Outside* magazine has been released. The cover is a collage of the prom-ised 'Outsiders of the Year' and bottom left there is one of Harry Borden's photos. It is just Mabel – admittedly looking rather beautiful, but most certainly her and her alone. I feel comfortable that Olive won't necessarily care, but I will make sure that she isn't able to log on to the internet this evening just in case.

Wednesday 18 November

One thing you discover about videos which have gone viral is that they have a very, very long life indeed. I have seen it in the past where somebody will have sent me a video or a GIF or a meme which is doing the rounds and I will recognise it from years before. Again, in this respect they are like human viruses – you might think they have died away, only for them to resurface in some corner of the world a few years later. Which is a cheering thought.

Well, today one of the Olive and Mabel originals (and, by sheer numbers, the biggest) was resurrected. I notice on Twitter that I am receiving two very different types of message from people in the United States. Some are saying things like 'THEFT! Credit @mrandrewcotter for this' while others are exclamations along the lines of 'Hell yeah!! THAT's what I'm talking about!!' and 'The win is going to be SWEET WHEN IT COMES', as if people have just decided to shout at me the kind of motivational nonsense you might get from a personal trainer, or somebody called Zane leading a spin class. But the clue to the actual reason lies in another Twitter account to which some of these people are also replying.

Dan Scavino Junior is one of the White House Deputy Chiefs of Staff and, following the modus operandi of his boss, is a fairly active chap on social media. As I discover, he has tweeted the video known as 'Game of Bones' – the one where I commentated on Mabel patiently waiting for her moment to steal the orange rubber bone from Olive. Now, Dan has simply taken the video and put it out himself where it has accrued over one million views, yet some ardent Olive and Mabel fans have tagged me in, bringing it to my attention and asking what I think. What I think is that the more than 20 million who viewed it in its original form in April will have seen it as no more than a funny bit of dog action with sports-style commentary. If it were satire, it was only a very seldom-used satire on sports broadcasters being out of work. Yet now this viral video has mutated. It has developed into a different strain, being served up as an allegory for the presidential election and the many followers of Scavino are firmly behind the idea that the bone is the election, Olive – as Joe Biden – has stolen it and Mabel – as Trump – will eventually get what is rightfully hers. As one of the least vain and most generous and friendly creatures I can imagine, this is poor casting of Mabel. Her hair is also rock solid in a strong breeze.

I suppose the things that really irk me about this are taking a video without recognition of where it came from or who created it and, above all, using Olive and Mabel for this kind of message. I understand entirely now why certain bands have either distanced themselves from, or expressly forbidden, politicians from using their songs in campaign ads or as incidental music at political rallies.

This episode does, though, reveal how faithfully the followers of Olive and Mabel will defend the dogs and, more importantly, defend the innocent fun and silliness of the video. Poor old Scavino consequently finds himself under a fairly sustained attack from the Olive and Mabel army.

He relents by putting out the original video and crediting me as the creator of it. The downside of which is that many thousands of lively characters now view me as some sort of Trump visionary. The actor James Woods, who appears to have a fondness for matters to the right of centre, has followed up on the Scavino message – and this Olive and Mabel video is now playing out on his account with a similar theme: Mabeltrump has been cheated...CHEATED of the bone. But don't worry folks – she gets it in the end and all is right (in so many ways) with the world.

As a result, my own following now swells with people who have a variety of stars and stripes, bald eagles and MAGA slogans adorning their accounts. Suddenly the troubles and conflicting issues of humans have infiltrated this harmless dog world which I tried to make as an escape from all of that. Indeed, looking at Mabel now, the only issue which appears to be troubling her is dealing with an itch on her knee, nose squashed up and teeth nibbling away.

I suppose the whole chapter is merely another reminder of how far Olive and Mabel have happily and unwittingly trotted out into our own world and all the problems and divisions that can be found there. If you had the inclination to study it more deeply, you could ask of the video: what is the original intention of the artist? And is that the only true meaning of it? Or, once a song, a novel, a film or a dog video is out there, can they be interpreted differently by people who can subsequently take from them anything they wish?

I do eventually put out a tweet, explaining to anybody

who will listen, from either side of the argument, that Mabel's original intention was that she just really, *really* wanted to have that rubber bone.

Friday 20 November

Have travelled back to London today as I am commentating on England versus Ireland at Twickenham tomorrow in the Autumn Nations Cup – a hastily cobbled together tournament to replace the usual visits of countries such as Australia and New Zealand, both of which are now boarded up and adrift somewhere in the southern seas.

Fiji have been included in the competition since many of their players are based in Europe but, as it happens, many of those players have also tested positive for coronavirus, so every single one of their matches is cancelled. This is how sport takes place at the moment – all of us uncertain that it is actually going to happen until the whistle blows, such is the tightrope we walk with cases rising rapidly and squads creating a relatively friendly environment for spreading if the virus should infiltrate. Therefore, along with the usual news of knee or shoulder injuries, there are regular updates on testing procedures and high temperatures with assurances that any positive tests will result in the player in question being swiftly removed from the team hotel and exiled to a small island in the Hebrides while all of their clothes are burned.

The serious nature and drastic measures taken do

remind us that sport is, after all, an important business and that in very difficult times, one slip can affect the livelihoods of so many people involved. What's more, television companies have paid significant money to the Unions who, without spectators buying tickets, rely on that income for their funding. On which note, this tournament has been my first time plying my trade on Prime Video, the television arm of Amazon. And so there it is…it's official – I have become part of the machine. Jeff Bezos is effectively now a work colleague and I look forward to getting drunk and badgering him for a pay rise at the office party.

Similar to the players and officials, we too have to go through any number of procedures before we are allowed to work – taking tests during the week and once again carrying a 'permission to travel' letter. This I keep in the glove box, secretly hoping to be stopped by a police officer at Warwick services who will flash a torch into the car and demand to see my papers. Sadly, no such dramatic incident occurs.

I actually have two equally redundant letters, since I am making the trip more than worth my while by throwing in an appearance on Radio 4's *Loose Ends*, a magazine programme which brings together great artistic talents and other guests who might just be at the centre of something quirky (guilty). But all of whom are connected by the common thread of having products which they would quite like to tell people about.

The recording takes place today at Broadcasting House, not far from Oxford Circus, in the art deco building which has been the headquarters of the BBC since the early 1930s. It has recently been expanded and brought up to date with a new extension, which houses what I am reliably informed is the largest live newsroom in the world. Although, rather like the hotel in Belfast, tonight there appear be two or three people on duty dealing with all the news that our planet has to offer and I am led through empty corridors by the pro gramme producer before a quick hello to the previous guest, Ian Hislop, editor of *Private Eye*, long-time pan-ellist on *Have I Got News For You* and also, I notice, one of the few people alive to wear a Homburg hat. I briefly ponder whether this is the kind of thing I should have tried to carry off at the *Mastermind* recording.

Soon inside the studio, I am ready to have a chat with Sara Cox and regular programme host Clive Anderson, two of the finest broadcasters around. Sara has that ease of chat – no affectation, no artificial broadcaster persona, just an ability to be herself on-air. And also to be very funny. Clive has had a long and stellar career, built upon a razor wit and the vast brain of a barrister – by which I mean his own, rather than one he keeps in a jar as a good-luck charm. And I'm very glad that his wit is not in adversarial mode here. I feel that I can keep up and hold my own in most conversations, but on occa-sion there is no shame at all in realising that you are a

Red Setter chatting to a Border Collie and simply wag your tail a bit in an endearing fashion.

In the past, Clive's often acerbic chat has reduced Richard Branson to pouring water over him (although Branson has done this with a few other people, it may just be a thing of his) and prompted the Bee Gees to storm off his television chat show in the 1990s – initially Barry, who didn't take well to the lively badinage, closely followed by Robin and then a slightly bemused and apologetic Maurice.

But here we are in the more forgiving environment of a gentle, easy-going, canine-based conversation.

'Where are the real stars, the dogs?' asks Clive, just before we start recording and my hand, if only for a moment, stretches out towards the glass in front of me.

Sunday 29 November

Nothing else to report today except that it is Olive's birthday. Eight years old and yet it seems so recently that we gathered up a small, black bundle to take home. I know these should just be joyful occasions – she is still near enough in her prime: sprightly, hale and hearty – but I always hear the ticking of the clock. Learn lessons from your dogs, I tell myself, enjoy the moment; don't mark the passage of time. Don't dwell on memories or look too far ahead. So much easier said…

I do occasionally worry that I am too strongly attached to them. Perhaps I should remind myself of how annoying they can sometimes be. Or even engineer an enormous falling-out where we don't speak to each other for weeks.

As it is, I try to film a birthday sketch where Mabel and I have planned a surprise party, but it's impossible to create an element of the unexpected when Olive knows full well that we are both behind the sofa – in particular when one of those hiding is whining excitedly and making the yucca plant rustle with a wagging tail. So in the end I just film Olive receiving an extra biscuit and even more attention than normal. And then of course Mabel too, because in the simple yet somehow very wise heads of dogs, this is just another day.

DECEMBER 2020

Thursday 3 December

The build-up to Christmas – which I believe now has an official start date of 14 August – has always been tortuous. We are assaulted by the same songs and further beaten into submission by the same advertisements, which all come with the same promise: that buying stuff will make everything OK. There is also the same insistence that by law you must be happy because Christmas is coming and…well, it's just amazing. And if you don't agree that it is amazing then there is obviously something wrong with you.

The TV commercials do prompt my brain into some sort of action though, as I decide to fashion a parody of a perfume ad, starring Olive and Mabel.

In terms of time taken from thinking of an idea for a video, to actually putting it out, this one has one of the shortest and simplest turnarounds. Others will require larger elements of production and dog direction, which is never the easiest aspect to manage. Too often you are desperately hoping that Olive and Mabel will do what you want of them in terms of sitting, staying or chatting away as their ears and tails come to life. But in this one I am a maverick director from the school of radical improvisation, simply releasing them on the beach at Formby and making use of whatever freestyle performance they produce.

In fact, the only stress was in trying to get there in time for a tiny rain-free weather window with darkness not too far away. But in the end it is ideal. I film everything in slow motion as the dogs run, brawl, dig frantically in the sand, chew a rubber ball or lick their noses and sniff the air – all in the watery half-light of a winter evening, with the last of the sun flickering on the sea and the occasional seagull lazily riding the wind and drifting past.

As I examine the footage back at home, I realise that, quite apart from anything else, the shots I have filmed are going to be nice memories of them both long after they have taken their final walk. But the rest of the job has still to be done, so I write and voice a suitably pretentious script, choose some music and a few sound effects, and let my regular video collaborator Tony Mabey work some of his magic on the edit. He's only been working on *Songs of Praise* so is glad of the distraction.

It looks beautiful. And quite apart from being a decent enough pastiche of perfume commercials, it seems to reflect my mood – the way this time of year can make you feel, as so many of us no doubt believe that we are living in our own film noir.

So out it goes. And I stir my coffee, slowly, until a small eddy starts to form on the surface. I tap the spoon twice with a clink on the edge of the cup and glance at the rain. Olive stares, seemingly at nothing – an indefinable point somewhere far beyond the window and the drops which trickle and weave their way down the glass, ending their journey in a gathering pool on the sill outside.

Mabel sighs.

Fin.

Saturday 5 December

At Twickenham again today, as England play France in the final of the Autumn Nations Cup – this last part of the tournament now misnamed as winter has officially begun and the weather is suitably chill and overcast. Walking round inside the giant concrete bowl of 80,000 empty seats, once more there is the recognition that this is sport only as a faint shadow of what it more usually offers. But it is something nonetheless and since we are currently feeding on scraps of entertainment and morsels of work, we will gladly accept it.

Not too long before kick-off, to add to this muted feeling, comes the news that Peter Alliss has died. Of course it shouldn't be a shock, given his age, but it somehow still is, probably because we were working together just last month. Possibly also because his presence seemed to be one of permanence, even if the last few months have dismissed the idea of such a concept.

Defying the sombre mood, the rugby which follows makes every effort to lift us – comfortably the best we have seen in the tournament. My powers of identification are sorely tested as France are forced to field a host of less familiar names and England win with the equally unfamiliar sight of a penalty to decide it in extra-time. Flames explode around the ground, the trophy is presented amidst the drifting smoke and tickertape and the stadium announcer turns the volume up to eleven, selling the moment to all those thousands of fans who are somewhere else.

I drive back up the road imagining the real noise of sport and the sound of life as it was. And remembering a voice from sunnier days.

Tuesday 8 December

So it begins. We have moved the initial teaspoon of earth in digging the tunnel which will get us out of here – the first Covid vaccination has been administered in the UK. Margaret Keenan, a week short of her ninety-first birthday, has the injection in a low-key setting at a hospital in Coventry where only she, the nurse and fourteen television crews are present. The first man to receive it is a chap called Bill Shakespeare, which does sound as if he has panicked and given a false name under the pressure of it all. But there is a feeling that the end may be in sight. Still a very long journey away, but we can perhaps see how we are going to get there.

This evening I take part in an online event with a bookseller in the United States, which is a very pleasant affair – some North American Olive and Mabel fans with a chance to see them snuffling at the camera or more often just lying on the sofa beside me while we all talk about dogs and how wonderful they are. A few hundred people have come along after a link to the event was put out on social media – the disadvantage of which is made clear within a few minutes while I am reading a lightly humorous passage from the book and a whole host of new guests joins the session. Suddenly, alongside the smiling faces of the good folk of Minnesota and beyond, enjoying a glass of Chablis with nibbles and dips, come attendees with usernames that even a fully paid-up member of the Klan in the 1950s might call 'a bit extreme'. There is also one newcomer who switches on his camera to reveal himself sprawling naked and enjoying the book discussion in a way that was not necessarily intended. Olive briefly raises her head at the commotion and Mabel carries on sleeping, galloping around in her innocent dreams. I try not to break stride either as I move seamlessly on to the challenges of the writing process.

Sunday 13 December

Hot on the heels of Olive turning eight, Mabel has her birthday today – junior dog is now four years old. In the very unscientific poll, her birthday announcement on social media achieves about twenty per cent more likes than that of Olive – ageism is a well-recognised problem in our industry. Following on from the American magazine cover incident, Olive would be justified in suffering a grievous blow to her confidence. Although as it is, she doesn't appear to give a toss.

Monday 14 December

Olive and Mabel storm the United States. In the greatest cultural invasion since Ed Sullivan introduced four lads from Liverpool, the piece we filmed finally appears on *Good Morning America*. There had been a few weeks of delay as every time it was scheduled to be shown, something to do with the aftermath of the presidential election kept getting in the way and took priority in their news coverage. But now they have decided that their daily light-hearted segment can return – the one where all three presenters raise an eyebrow or two, offer a wall of perfectly white teeth and banter gently in and out of the segment as if they are all the very best friends in the world. Tomorrow it might be a cat who learned how to surf, or a hamster that has translated Proust, but today it is the story of our two dogs. So out it goes and we are on-air, coast to coast, across the nation. Our fame is now unlimited.

'Meet Mabel and Olive, the viral pups!' comes the attendant blurb. 'With owner, travelling sportscaster Andrew Conner!'

It's close enough.

Tuesday 15 December

Question: What can one possibly do to add stress to your life when you already feel that you are operating at peak stress capacity?

Answer: Move house.

I would like to make clear that it wasn't our decision to throw this into the mix at this specific time – our house has been on the market for a couple of years. But clearly a lot of people are deciding that the combination of the removal of a huge chunk of stamp duty plus an overwhelming desire for a change of scene is enough to spur them into action.

I have not been stressed so much as a bit emotional about leaving. Moving on...change... It always affects me quite strongly.

You are, of course, supposed to look forward – bounding into the future like a chocolate Labrador, with the firm belief that everything can and will get better and life is but a series of improvements. Which of course isn't really the case. It is just a series of different stages and when one of those stages has been very happy, there is always going to be a feeling of regret that you are closing that chapter. It is a reminder of the passage of time and comes with a sensation that a part of you is being left behind.

Added to that was the emotion of the past year and the fact that everything Olive and Mabel-related has happened here in this house. They might only be silly videos but many, many millions of people have seen that slightly grubby patio where they inhaled their food. Or that corner of the sitting room by the windows where Olive lost possession of an orange bone. Or the cramped office in which I recorded a Zoom meeting, or the pond a hundred yards away in which Mabel had pointlessly stood and stared.

I feel I should perhaps contact those who install the blue plaques on houses where great achievers have lived, so that one might be put up on the outer wall, reading *'Olive and Mabel. Dogs who did stuff on the internet. Lived and worked here 2013–2020'.*

With our two most treasured possessions of all sitting upright in their beds in the boot of my car, my thoughts are largely of them and how they were brought here as puppies and settled in so quickly. This has been their home – they knew where their comfortable places were to be found, they knew the kitchen and where to gather for biscuits before bedtime. They knew the neighbours and knew that they deeply hated one of their cats. They knew every nook and cranny, every sniff of this house. Now they won't be back here again and I wonder if it will register with them at all.

But we try to be positive and look to the future, thinking only of making that move forward. I'm sure they will be content as long as they are with us and vice versa. Yes, this has been a very happy home for all of us, but the next one can be as well. So we look on as our other possessions are taken away, and we have that certainty that they are only items – just objects. It is the memories we have made which are by far the most important things to keep. I am contemplating all of this as the removal van reverses off down the narrow lane, steadily veers off course and gets stuck in a ditch.

Wednesday 16 December

Very concerned about Olive today. She is listless and doesn't want to get up at all. She stays in her bed, unable to be cajoled into doing anything and only when summoned for dinner does she make an effort to haul herself up and then walks very slowly indeed to her bowl, as if driven by a primal force deep within telling her that this is what she simply has to do, no matter how bad she feels. But I know she is only operating on autopilot. If she keeled over and died on me right there, that Labrador spirit would no doubt rise from the body, look around briefly and then carry on floating towards the bowl of food.

I've read about depression in dogs and having checked out the symptoms on a veterinary website, it seems very possible that she really is in a state of deep melancholy; perhaps it is as I feared and she is pining for the only home she has known for the eight years of her life and where she has felt comfortable. It's surely too much of a coincidence that this transformation in her mood has occurred the day after we move house.

Such is our panicky, overprotective way, I ring the vet and am told that they only have urgent appointments available and can I explain a little more about the emergency nature of the injury or illness of the dog in question?

I tell her that she seems a bit glum.

'Right. Call back in the morning.'

So a fretful night passes while I sleep on the sofa near to Olive, stroking her head. And occasionally try to lift her spirits by telling a couple of amusing stories.

Thursday 17 December

Little improvement in Olive this morning and so I am now certain it is serious. Because if there's one thing that both she and Mabel do quite superbly at the start of each day it is joyful idiocy, running around telling everyone that today is going to be great, it really is. Give us food and then get ready for a great day. Which will be great, in case I hadn't mentioned that. But now Olive remains resolutely hangdog, head low and tail down.

I have spent most of the year seeing these dogs as role models – paragons of blind optimism in the face of adversity. But if even one of our upbeat morale officers has finally been ground down by life then what hope is there for the rest of us?

Thankfully the vet does have an appointment for later that day and when we arrive, Olive is no better. At least with Covid regulations she doesn't have to go through the stress of sitting in the waiting room. Instead we call a number and somebody comes out to the car – it's effectively a drive-thru vet where you hold a dog up to the window and describe the symptoms. As ever, when presented with an actual medical professional, I feel the need to assist them with my own poorly thought-out diagnosis.

'I think she might be a little depressed.'

'Hmmm…right… It's probably *not* that, but we'll have a look.'

So Olive is led in, tail still between legs and I am left to sit in the car, worrying and conjuring up all manner of dark thoughts, while another vet at the drive-thru chats through a car window to the owner of a small, frizzy dog which appears to have a mild cough.

Fifteen minutes later and another black Labrador is brought out, pulling at her lead and straining to get to me. But it is Olive. Utterly transformed – and the reason is quite simple.

'She had a bit of a bad back,' comes the diagnosis, as Olive leaps athletically into the boot of the car. 'It was all locked up so we just had to loosen it off.'

And there it is – a bit of manipulation from the vet and a few minutes of properly applied massage has made the world of difference. In addition, we are given a course of anti-inflammatory medication which we have to drizzle over her food like a jus. 'Sometimes the taste of it can be off-putting,' says the vet and I assure her that this really won't be an issue, as you could pour kerosene over her kibble and she wouldn't notice until stepping too close to a naked flame. But already Olive is moving easily and looking quite chipper – ears up and tail back where it should be, waving around happily as my bank card is requested and I feel my own spirits sag and back tighten.

I know I have probably overreacted throughout the whole thing but I understand again something of what it must be like to have children – the feeling of protection and wanting, *needing* to make everything OK is overwhelming. But, of course, with a child I could have asked them to help me out in being a bit more specific about what was ailing them. Much of this stress and worry would have been avoided if Olive could simply have said, 'God no, LOVE this new place. Tell you what, though, my lumbago isn't half playing up.' It is another salutary lesson that while we might believe we know exactly what our dogs are saying, thinking or feeling, often we haven't got the slightest clue.

So we return home and to a far more contented evening for everyone. Olive is curled up and sighing happily – her back feels better and all is fine with the world again. What's more, she's absolutely off her face on drugs and loving it.

Sunday 20 December

New rules come into place for London and the southeast of England. Such is the escalation of Covid cases in this region that millions of people are effectively under a new lockdown and not allowed to travel to other parts of the country. Everybody seems to deal with the news stoically. Maintaining that stoicism as they stoically gather their family, pack up their cars and stoically get out of London, heading to other parts of the country. Footage of London railway terminals shows thousands crowding to get onto trains. I'm sure this will all be absolutely fine.

Tuesday 22 December

Just past the shortest day – the scant daylight hours are combining with wretched weather to ensure that it never really gets light at all. Night has fallen by approximately midday and this time of year – which has always tended towards the dark and difficult – is doing its insidious work again. You can understand why various religions decided to arrange their major uplifting social events for this part of the calendar. Anything to help. I wish my own mood could be cured in such a way – or perhaps by a biscuit from the vet, heavily laced with anti-inflammatories.

Fortunately we have the mind and time-occupying fuss and work of transplanting ourselves into a new home – maybe it's not a bad thing to be going through this now, after all. But the rain is relentless and everywhere has turned to the mud and mush of a windy and wet winter. Plague, war and now floods – the various horsemen of the apocalypse are saddling up. So how can we counter it? For many people who are not otherwise distracted by shifting the contents of one house to another, the solution appears to be to buy a dog.

In fact, even in normal years, this time of year is recognised as one best avoided when it comes to buying a dog. An ill thought-out or panic purchase as a Christmas present – the recipient finding out by January, or possibly even late afternoon on 25 December, that they are profoundly unprepared for the demands of canine ownership and the effort required, but also then discovering that you can't return them like a pair of jeans which are a fraction too long on the inside leg. So instead they are dropped off at shelters. Or, far worse, just abandoned.

This is why the cautionary message has always been, 'A dog is for life, not just for Christmas.' But now people are not only buying dogs for Christmas they are doing it whenever – a dog is for Christmas, Hanukkah, Father's Day, Eid, the birthday of former *Happy Days* actor Henry Winkler – anything. It's entirely understandable given what we are all going through – shut down in our houses, we crave something different, something to take our focus away from all the problems and all of the tension – some light-hearted diversionary entertainment.

And so, enter the dogs...

This might put a great deal of pressure on our canine accomplices – the idea that they could be the saviours of humankind, or at least the saviours of their sanity. If they had any idea, they would probably be chain-smoking in the room next door like a comedian waiting in the wings – a French bulldog slapping its face with its paws and giving itself a pep talk. 'Right, come on, Alan – you can do this. The humans have had a rough day with work and family... It's up to you. *Showtime...*' just before wandering out into the sitting room and rolling around on its back while chewing a rubber Garfield toy. But, of course, the dogs don't know. They are blissfully unaware of what's going on or what sort of human pressures we might be under and for that they are all the better.

Their appearance fees, however, are now astronomical. It's quite simple – the basic laws of supply and demand mean that the price of desirable breeds is rocketing. Puppies are currently subject to their own super-inflation, like the Dutch tulip mania of the seventeenth century. Unscrupulous people are putting a fur coat on a tortoise and hoping nobody will notice that their new schnauzer is a bit lethargic.

You hope that some of those thinking about a dog would consider rehoming a rescue, for any number of reasons, but I suppose they are understandably scared off by the baggage sometimes carried by those ill-treated beasts and the extra care that might therefore be required. Besides, people are easily led by fashions and trends, so instead, a few select breeds or exotic new blends take all the custom.

Consider, for example, the Cavapoo. Not yet an officially recognised breed, this unfortunately named creature is a cocktail of Cavalier King Charles spaniel and poodle and is fairly small, but has a perky nature as well as the endearing and inquisitive face of an Ewok from *Star Wars*.

Another of its key features is that it is considered hypoallergenic, so it appeals to people who might be reduced to a snuffling, watery-eyed mess at the mere mention of a dog. Interestingly (and I suppose I should really let you be the judge on this claim), there is some debate about whether hypoallergenic dog breeds exist at all and that the factors which cause allergies are more or less prevalent in individual dogs, rather than particular breeds.

It is certainly a myth that there are breeds of dogs that don't shed fur. All dogs shed. It's just that some, like poodles, have wiry coats that keep even the loosened fur in place and don't therefore have it floating around them in a cloud, like Mabel, who gets her own back on her nemesis vacuum cleaners by working them constantly until they finally submit, clogged by a million blonde furs, and can whirr no more.

This is also why there are a vast number of dogs now containing more than a pinch of poodle in their DNA mixture: schnoodles, goldendoodles, cockapoos, sproodles, bernedoodles, yorkipoos, maltipoos, poochons to name but a few. Dog lists are currently full of portmanteau titles and I'm not sure quite how some of them have been achieved, as it must have involved considerable gymnastic ability for the participants, or at the very least some sort of stepladder.

Of course, most breeds created over the last couple of hundred years are themselves blends – we just used to be slightly more creative with the names. But what is clear is that poodles are now taking over – a dominance secured solely, it seems, by the thought that they have magic, human-friendly coats. So numerous are they becoming that there is a chance the future of Earth is not that vision seen in *Planet of the Apes* where we are subservient to simians, but instead a world where poodle variants rule – having overthrown us with little trouble, as they were able to sneak up without giving the game away by making us sneeze.

And yet, I feel compelled to mention that, despite the rise of contenders from the poodle-infused masses, the world's most popular breed of dog remains the Labrador. Which, taken to its logical if somewhat speculative conclusion, means that by approximately the year 2097 the pre-eminent creature on Earth will be the Labradoodle.

What a kindly, happy and utterly clueless planet we will then be.

Friday 25 December

It is a quiet Christmas. As was always going to be the case.

Until the decision a few days ago, it did appear that we might be able to have one family member to stay, but the border between Scotland and England is effectively now closed to all except Amazon delivery drivers, and my mother is unable to travel. She accuses me of having a contact in the higher levels of government and calling in a favour.

So, if not quite a silent night it is certainly low-key, which is not in any way a hardship. And, such is the way of things and the new order of importance in our pack, Olive and Mabel seem to be receiving more presents than anybody else. Most of them edible, to their great delight. Some of them wearable, to less evident pleasure.

Olive is offered a bright red scarf, which was her present three or four years ago, but we are re-gifting. Her expression when it is unwrapped in front of her carries none of the feigned enthusiasm that will doubtless be on display around the land from disappointed humans today – dogs being utterly incapable of white lies. Her expression says less, 'Ooh *lovely*, just what I wanted...' and more, 'What on earth is this shit and where is the selection box of dog treats that I've been dropping obvious hints about for the last few weeks?' In the end, though, she reluctantly agrees to have the scarf put on and thereafter sports it with good grace – secretly I think she knows that she looks good in it. I do worry for a moment that she might remember it from a previous Christmas and be hurt that we haven't got her something new, before reminding myself that she won't do either of those things, because she's a dog. Mabel is briefly put in a hat, which remains on her head for whatever the unit of time is just below a micro-second. Eventually she tolerates being adorned with a garland of tinsel around her neck and that is more than enough – looking at social media I feel a great deal of sympathy for dogs in knitwear up and down the country tonight.

Unable to be here in person, my mother sends an out of focus, slightly lop-sided photo of her bullmastiff, Mungo, wearing a set of reindeer antlers and even through the blur you can see that his eyes carry a blend of nobility, sadness and a real hope that Christmas will be over soon. In which matter he speaks for many of us.

Monday 28 December

Woke up to quite a sight this morning, as there has been a landslide in the garden – the constant rain and occasional snow of recent weeks taking its toll on a steep slope which comes down from a field. To be honest we are just grateful that a tree or some unsuspecting livestock hasn't descended with it. Both Olive and Mabel trot over the top of the debris, sniffing away at the new feature fashioned from tons of clay soil. As with most things, Mabel manages to look both guilty and apologetic – but I reassure her, saying that I know this wasn't caused by any vigorous digging in the flowerbed.

This can all be considered part of the adjustment as both dogs get used to their new surroundings. Not only the house and shape-shifting garden, but new walks in the vicinity which are, of course, the only outings we can make at the moment.

The forest nearby has become our late-night expedition, when we frequently seem to have it to ourselves. Nothing to disturb us but the one or two-note song of an owl from somewhere in the dark and the huge pine trees which tower over the trails and sway and creak in the wind – the moonlight filtering through the branches and faintly illuminating Mabel who sticks close by, clipping at my heels, while Olive stalks along unseen in her own world of nocturnal investigation. You could easily think it an eerie place – there is a reason why so many sinister fairy tales are set in the enclosing murk of a Germanic forest – but for me it is nothing but peaceful. Likewise, Olive is perfectly relaxed, free to chew away at any number of unpleasant things without me catching her in the act, while Mabel is more on edge, occasionally startled by the noise of a small, unidentified creature scurrying away through the foliage. Everybody's mind works in a different way and our imagination creates all manner of different things – even when that mind is operating at a very low voltage.

Meanwhile their regular short walk looks as if it will be up and down a nearby lane which, at first glance, doesn't seem to offer much in the way of stimulation, but today I discovered offers plenty of excitement. As I firmly believed that the fields on either side were empty, both were off their leads and busying themselves with all sorts of crucial dog matters. And I was busying myself with any amount of nonsense in my head and consequently paying very little attention.

I turned round to see only Mabel remaining and, despite heavy interrogation, she was unable to offer any information as to where her senior colleague had gone. But almost immediately the answer came with a harmony of happy dog expletives and slightly alarmed mooing, so a sprint was made to a gap in the hedge which revealed the sight of Olive and three cows involved in what appeared to be a freestyle canine–bovine dance-off. It was also clear to any neutral observer that Olive was winning – leaping and spinning around while the cows merely stared and lumbered uneasily backwards and forwards, knowing that they were outclassed but perhaps hoping for a favourable decision from the judges.

The competition, though, was brought to an abrupt end by a shout from me, my voice reaching a volume that I didn't know I possessed but also at the pitch of an audience at a K-pop concert. Olive is not often swayed by my interventions, but as the hysterical shockwaves reached her and blew her ears backwards, she realised that, on this occasion, she might have made a wrong decision. Above all I know two things: a farmer could legally pick her off like a sniper without any repercussion and furthermore, startled cows are incredibly dangerous in their sheer bulk, so I managed to combine both anger and a pleading tone, which did get Olive out of the field. Leaving the cows to resume chewing a bit of grass and working on their unimpressive dance moves.

As for the dogs, I marched them both straight home in disgrace. Olive staying close now, trotting alongside as I wasted my breath explaining the rationale behind the punishment.

'Yes, I know the walk is being cut short but maybe you'll think twice before dancing with cows again.'

Olive just stared blankly. Mabel apologised on behalf of everybody involved.

Thursday 31 December

Here we are again – another year over. As ever, a time for reflection. A time for looking back on the year past and gazing ahead to whatever might lie in our clouded future.

It is impossible not to get emotional about all that has happened in the last twelve months. Remembering sitting on the summit of An Teallach on this day last year, contemplating the year ahead with a fair degree of confidence in how it would unfold – as most people would, wherever they might have been. We knew the people we would see, all the places we would go and the work we would do, but of course, as it turns out we didn't have a clue. For example, tonight I have filmed a piece for *The Big New Year's In* with Paddy McGuinness on BBC1 where I play Monopoly with my dogs.

The programme itself doesn't stand out – not least in that approximately ninety-five per cent of UK television programmes appear to be hosted by Paddy McGuinness now, but it is still something notable for Olive and Mabel to feature as part of it with a specially commissioned video.

It does bring a little bit of extra pressure as I am usually making the videos only for myself, although being part of a bigger machine certainly has its advantages. You see, sometimes the most difficult thing about making a video is in terms of the production and thinking about whether or not you are even allowed to feature certain items. *Monopoly*, for example, is a product and one which belongs to somebody else – in this case, the games company Hasbro. Of course, I could do as the vast majority of the uploading population do and just use any product, photos, videos or music they want and cleverly circumvent the awkward rights issue by using the loophole of not giving a flying toss. But I want to do the right thing. I also want to use the theme music for *Black Beauty* and if I were making a video purely by myself then this would just not be possible, as you simply can't purchase the rights to well-known pieces of music. With the BBC, though, there is a blanket rights deal, so near enough any piece of music ever written can be cleared. And whereas when I am making a video myself, I err on the side of caution, if you are working for a major company, there is somebody else to do the official worrying and checking for you. So with this, the BBC lawyers are consulted and they ask how the Monopoly board will be featured. The key considerations are: will it be in vision for long and will it be shown in a positive light? I tell them that one dog will be rolling the dice while another chews the hotels on Park Lane and Mayfair. And they seem comfortable with that.

Thus, given the green light, I film it – Olive and Mabel perform admirably and the piece is duly delivered. Then we settle down with millions of others to watch the dogs' prime-time appearance.

As the programme wends its merry way, I soon realise that Olive and Mabel playing board games doesn't really fit the tone. This feeling is endorsed by an accompanying live Twitter commentary from fans of the dogs, who are watching based only on the firm promise I had made that the stars were going to appear. As more and more of these observations come in, I note that they are not uniformly positive, but the feeling is that the Olive and Mabel followers are prepared to put up with it as they patiently wait for the reward of their favourite dogs.

Yet as 11 p.m. approaches, with Paddy wrapping things up and bidding us all a cheery Lancashire farewell, it becomes abundantly clear that Olive and Mabel have been dropped. Shortly after the credits roll, an email comes in from the executive producer, apologising and explaining that we were squeezed out because the live drag queen act went on longer than planned. I pass on this news to Mabel who looks as if there are any number of things about it that she doesn't really understand. Olive deals with the disappointment by continuing to sleep, upside down. Most frustratingly it now feels too late to change the piece, knowing that I would have to remove the *Black Beauty* music and purchase a similar-sounding replacement if I want to put it out on Twitter. But too much work has gone into it to let it slip away unseen – apart from anything else I bought a new game of Monopoly and a moderately priced travel chess set for this.

So I spur myself into action and Mabel scampers around with me, sensing some sort of urgency as if we are all in a bit of trouble, while Olive carries on snoring. With time against us, I rudely interrupt Tony's New Year's Eve since his editing fingers work like lightning while I could just about have it perfected by 17 January. Instead, he delivers in just a moment or two and it is out there with a few minutes of 2020 to spare.

It is a video which spends the middle part looking ahead with hopes and dreams for the new year from the dogs' point of view. Oh, to be as blissfully ignorant as they are, happy with their lot and also never peering

75

too far into the future beyond the next walk or dining arrangement. Although humans also seem to be wary of looking too far ahead this time. Usually this is a night where social media is overpopulated with accounts saying, 'This year is going to be MASSIVE' and 'Let's smash it in 2021 people!!' accompanied by the clenched fist emoji. But now the messages that come in are somewhat weary and often just shouting abuse at 2020.

There is also, though, an optimistic tone – a feeling that bidding farewell to this terrible year means that it's all going to improve and we can make a new start with a blanket New Year's resolution to go to the gym, quit smoking and stop having coronavirus. The notion, as the clock chimes midnight, is that suddenly everything will be different, that somehow it was 2020's fault, as if the pandemic might have been paying close attention to the Gregorian calendar.

The unspoken reality is that we are actually in the deep end as our second wave hits and still have some distance to go to wade, or doggy paddle, our way out.

So I say a cautious, but heartfelt Happy New Year to Olive, Mabel and Caroline. In that order.

She understands.

JANUARY 2021

Saturday 2 January

A new year and a new matter to occasionally occupy my thoughts as I've started writing a magazine column for a national newspaper.

'What is the column about?' you rather needlessly ask, as if I may have been granted an outlet to chat about North American politics or the latest developments in the world of haberdashery. But, of course, it is about dogs. As I freely admit in the first canine thought-piece which I file, this is what I do now. I am the dog man.

In the evening, our episode of *Mastermind* is finally broadcast and I hope that nobody has noticed – it is a somewhat chastening viewing experience. The first thing I realise on seeing myself floundering amidst the crossfire of questions, is that I squint my eyes as if in great pain when trying to think of an answer and I am also clearly in a state of some confusion as to what I should be doing with my legs. Throughout the interrogation I shift uneasily in the leather chair, moving from 'man returning from office party, reclining on last train home' to 'slightly camp gentleman hoping to impress at job interview'. I'm also reminded just how many questions I get wrong and above all hope that nobody will mention 'tin-gate'.

Almost as soon as the programme has finished, my phone pings with a message from one of my helpful brothers:

Did you not know that one about D.H. Lawrence?

To which I very nearly reply:

Why yes – I did know, but I decided the best thing to do would be to not answer and retain an air of mystery.

There then follows a great deal of correspondence from friends and acquaintances offering correct answers, with many of them simply a one-word message, saying 'PANINI'. People I haven't heard from in months, or years, or at all, are getting in touch to tell me things that I already know, since I had them seared onto my hippocampus by John Humphreys two months ago. If not that, they are gently enquiring as to why I was sitting like a cross between Mabel and Quentin Crisp. I reply to most of these messages that, while what they say may well be true, there are few people in the world who know more about *Bagpuss*.

At the end of the day, I make the mistake of flicking through Twitter before going to sleep – widely recognised as being bad for you both physically and very probably mentally as well. An unwise click on the hashtag #celebritymastermind reveals that everybody's performance is being discussed in the thorough and robust ways of social media. And so, the last things I see before I slip off to soothing dreams in the faraway land of nod are:

'Is there some sort of connection between being a celebrity and a MORON?' and 'It's TIN. Why doesn't he know it's TIN???'

Tuesday 5 January

Unable to sleep much last night. Which is a very common theme at the moment.

With my ongoing lack of sufficient slumber, I envy the dogs the thing which is perhaps their greatest talent. Not the ability to clean their own backside, as I consider that more of a burden than a gift. No, I wish that, like them, I were just able to sleep, deeply and instantly. I applaud the ability they have to switch off their brain – albeit with most breeds it is not exactly a laborious procedure. The checklist before they close their eyes is brief:

Am I warm and comfortable? Yes.

Am I fed? (Yes. Not enough, but yes).

Am I safe? Yes.

So the internal pronouncement 'All is well' is made and the lights are switched off in their heads. Perhaps with the extra security of a paw draped over a nose.

What a contrast with us. I fret about work, about the world, about anything and everything, and those troublesome thoughts dance around, subjects changing, head buzzing away. Must get on top of this, do that, deal with the other thing. What a contrast to the beautiful simplicity of the mind of a dog. Yes, they have their own small and at times very strange concerns, but generally they live by those three central questions.

Am I warm?

Am I fed?

Am I safe?

These can be arranged in a different order depending on the breed, but generally they seem to drive all dogs and dictate their levels of satisfaction with the world. I wish these answers were enough for me. They really should be.

When I did finally drift off last night, it was into a sleep dominated by a vivid dream about the landslide, but now everything – the whole garden, house and street – is being washed away. Whoever is directing my dreams is not a fan of subtlety in symbolism.

So, later in the morning I try and deal with some of the clutter in my head. I go outside and spoon a couple of spadefuls of mud away from a bush which appears to be choking. I then tap down a small bit of earth, making no discernible difference, but I do feel marginally better about life in general.

This leads me to briefly contemplate an Olive and Mabel gardening video – or perhaps a book along those lines to challenge the horticulture/dog-genre dominance of Monty Don, with the notion only grinding to a halt on the inconvenience of knowing next to nothing about gardening. I then pick up a couple of stray dog toys which, having been carried out with great enthusiasm the night before, have been casually abandoned. The famous orange rubber bone lies half hidden in a shrub of undetermined species. I offer them to both dogs asking them to carry them back in, but they look at me as if toy recovery is well below their pay grade.

I think I might have become slightly more obsessive about trying to tidy up and to have things just so. If I can maintain some sort of order in my home life then it offers a semblance of a feeling of control, at a time when we seem so utterly powerless in the rest of our lives. If the garden is cleared up it will help. If my sock drawer is neatly arranged then the pandemic isn't quite so bad.

In the afternoon I head into our nearest town to get a few things from the supermarket. To nobody's surprise at all, we are paying the price for our Christmas get-togethers with the country now returning to a state of full lockdown once more and, as this is my expedition for the day, I make the most of it by parking some distance away and taking a walk down the main street. In a bitterly cold wind and the half-light of January, the scene would be bleak enough, but now almost every door is closed to darkened shops behind – so many small and independent businesses with owners doubtless fretting over what might happen in the weeks and months to come. It's two o'clock on a Tuesday afternoon and there is scarcely a soul around. I do notice one person coming out of a hardware shop, pulling their coat closer to them as they step into the sleety rain which is starting to come down, so I head in there myself – not really needing anything but simply drawn to the light and any sign of life or vestige of normality.

Once there I drift aimlessly down the aisles, looking at items scattered around quite thinly stocked shelves while the store speakers play *Last Christmas*, as if reluctant to let it go. I pause at a selection of axes, furrowing my brow and picking one up, feeling the weight because it is my solemn duty as a man to give the impression that I know what I'm doing. I do momentarily consider that I might need one to chop up some of the wood in the garden, but think better of it, as even to my untrained eye they don't appear to be of the highest quality and, besides, a lone man walking down the empty high street while brandishing an axe would go too far in replicating a post-apocalyptic scene. So in the end I attempt to justify my visit by purchasing a couple of lightbulbs which I'm fairly sure have the wrong sort of connection and then I leave, heading off to the supermarket, moving quickly past the empty railway station and the platforms where nobody stands, waiting for trains that seldom come.

Saturday 9 January

The snow conditions in the Scottish mountains are extraordinarily good this winter. Or at least they would be good if I could get anywhere near them but, as it is, travel restrictions rule out the possibility. So in fact the snow conditions are neither good nor bad – they just are. And now I find myself taunted on social media by photos which are posted by people who live close enough to the hills to have this playground as an option for their daily walk allowance. It belongs to them and them alone. My envy knows no bounds.

This petty frustration is only increased by the pristine and empty nature of the digital visions sent my way. Like so many unreachable places, they are not only more desirable because of their unattainability, but because they have been somehow cleansed and are now closer to the ideal we have of them, or they exist more as they once were. Because, of course, in recent decades the world has become a very small and busy place. Travel is so easy and so cheap that nowhere is – or was – beyond our reach. It has become such an enormous part of our lives and we have always taken it for granted, even though mass movement is a fairly recent phenomenon in the whole strand of human progress.

Once upon a time, not that long ago, it was the preserve of the very wealthy or the very noble – often one and the same. It was only those fortunate, select few who were able to indulge in a Grand Tour, the name given to the trips that flourished in the eighteenth and early nineteenth centuries, whereby members of the upper class, upon coming of age, would take themselves around the great cities of Europe on jaunts which lasted months or even years because they didn't really have anything better to do. They might start in Paris and then find themselves languishing for a while in Italy, being schooled in Classical Antiquity or the Renaissance in Rome, Florence or Venice, before travelling back through the Alps, to Munich or Heidelberg and then Amsterdam, eventually returning to some enormous pile in England and filling it with appropriated knick-knacks or a few paintings of themselves looking suitably noble in a variety of locations. The expeditions were presented as vital in furthering a young man's education (for it was only men initially), even though they seem more like the antecedent of a modern gap year – i.e. largely arsing about and delaying the prospect of finding a job.

The popularity of these trips (for those who had the means) was spread through the writings of travellers such as Boswell – the faithful adjutant and biographer of Samuel Johnson – or even the great Romantic poet and general pleasure-seeker Lord Byron who, as he did with most things, took his holidays to excess and spent years traipsing around Portugal, Spain, Italy and Turkey, along the way managing to throw himself wholeheartedly into a variety of earthly distractions as well as the Greek War of Independence.

Another tourist was the less aristocratic but far more wealthy William Beckford, who had inherited such riches from his father's sugar plantations (along with approximately three thousand slaves), that he could enlist Mozart as a music teacher and Alexander Cozens to show him how to hold a paintbrush. Among his multitude of passions, he might also be considered one of the first travel writers – using those fortunes to spend a comfortable year musing about life in Italy, before settling down again in Wiltshire where he displayed a penchant for architecture in constructing large and occasionally very unstable buildings.

If these were the early travel influencers then the mass participation really began with the invention of the steamship and the spread of the railways, ensuring that many more could follow in the footsteps of those select few. But still as recently as the second half of the twentieth century, explorers had places as yet undiscovered and mountains largely unseen let alone unclimbed. It is really only in the past three or four decades that we have travelled in such vast numbers – air travel taking us further and cheaper than ever before.

Naturally, it is a wonderful thing that tourism is no longer the preserve of the tiny minority and is instead available to so many more. But it does tend to mean that when we reach those places, we realise that we are not the only people who might have had that idea. So many of us now in the developed world have the time and the means to travel and we dream of those weeks when we can do so. Online, on television or in print we see the image and decide that we would like to be there, but when we reach the destination find that it doesn't really exist. Or at least not exactly as promised in the picture.

You might hope to take a quiet stroll around the Uffizi or marvel at the Valley of the Kings where, along with the tombs of pharaohs, you would see the scratched Greek or Latin graffiti of ancient sightseers, which reminds us that tourism has long been part of the human experience. But it has never been quite so overwhelming. Perhaps travel further afield to Machu Picchu, trek to Everest, or gaze in awe at the spiritual and otherworldly Uluru. And they can be presented as we imagine them to be – but just out of shot, beyond the cropped edges of the photo, will be the dozens all waiting to have their moment and their version of the ideal, or a cameraman filming the lower reaches of the Khumbu Ice Fall for Google Street View. No corner of the globe remains untouched or uncaptured which, depending on your point of view, is either marvellous or is something lost forever. The easier it is to travel, the more we lack any sense of mystery and true adventure.

Yet a hint of that unknown and a glimpse of the untouched have now returned, since mass travel has come to a grinding halt. So if you were somehow able to travel to these places today, you would be stepping back in time. And while that brings the obvious frustration that we can't be there, it does mean that those sights, the wonders of our world, can rest – they are the overworked fields that now get a chance to lie fallow and recover. Of course, when the world opens up we'll celebrate our freedom and we'll travel again and we will swarm to those places and once more suffocate the things which we love. But for now at least, they breathe.

Until that time where we can move, I have decided to go on a muting spree of various outdoorsy-based accounts which I follow so that I don't have to be tormented by the pure, untainted views. But now I am contemplating the fact that travel IS still permitted for essential work, a loophole which was used to great effect over the festive period when flights to Dubai seemed to be filled entirely with influencers claiming that they were heading there on business, but in reality posted only one photo of a glass of wine on a beach or a selfie while riding a camel. And for just a moment I wonder again how essential the work of Olive and Mabel videos might be considered.

But, of course, I don't take things any further than a fleeting thought. Even if I know I will not come into contact with anybody and possibly not even see another soul on a trip into the mountains, I am hamstrung by an eagerness to do the right thing and also by an enormous fear of authority. A police officer only has to glance in my direction for me to wonder how I might have transgressed. In that, I am far more like Mabel than Olive, who would simply stare down the representative of the law and ask them what the hell did they think they were looking at.

So now, my vision of being alone in the hills has no chance of winning in this guilty mind. One which is already imagining a scenario where somebody posts a picture of the three of us out and about, or I'm caught on CCTV, looking round furtively as I release Olive and Mabel for a comfort break at Tebay services on the M6. 'BAD DOGS...' runs the headline in a couple of papers while another, more creative, goes for 'WHO LET THE DOGS OUT?' and the story gathers pace.

I am shamed on social media and take an opportunity to return to *BBC Breakfast* and explain myself in an exercise of damage control. 'It's the only work I have,' I protest, brandishing a statement from YouTube indicating the £5.80 which my mountain video has accumulated. But this is now a far graver version of Louise Minchin, who only shakes her head, says the viewers can make up their own minds before handing sadly to the weather.

No, I'll just take the dogs for their own grand tour of the nearby lane instead.

Monday 11 January

I am in the process of building a home gym. This pleases me.

Caroline has raised the valid point that perhaps firstly we should try to furnish the house, making the very reasonable argument that having chairs to sit upon is more important than a free-weights rack. I duly noted her concerns a couple of days ago, before informing her that twenty-five square metres of rubber flooring would be arriving in the 7 a.m. to 9 a.m. time slot if she could listen out for the door.

In the current situation, with all such commercial facilities closed, the need for a home gym is obvious to me. In fact, I think I might have proceeded down this route even without a pandemic to prod me along. While a fairly dedicated gym attendee for all of my adult life, I had started to go off them before the viral fun began. This was due to the fact that my most recent gym seemed to latterly consist almost entirely of dark rooms with pumping music and neon lettering telling me this was the new Zzappp!!! activity zone, or some such thing, a revolutionary form of exercise started by an ex-US Marine in San Diego called Doug who was using it as a means of combatting his anger management issues, and that my subscription had gone up as a result.

Since all I wanted to do, in my old school ways, was get on a treadmill or move some metal objects from one place to another and then back again, I finally relinquished my membership at the start of 2020, although a year later I do still occasionally receive a text or email asking me if I am absolutely certain about my decision. Which I am, because in case I failed to mention it, I'm building my own home gym.

I have given it that grand title, but it's effectively just that I have laid the flooring in the garage and bought an inflatable ball. I do also have some kettlebells but they are non-threatening in size and sit, in assorted pastel colours, in the corner. So I decided to buy some more dumbbells and today, the first task is to pretend that I am having no problem at all lifting the box out of the van when they're delivered.

'Sure you can manage?' says the driver.

'Not a problem, pal,' as I slip unconvincingly into customer–tradesman banter. 'Have you got the ten Ks as well there, fella?'

'Those are the ten Ks. The twenty-five Ks are here.'

After this exchange, my very good mate then tells me that all he is delivering at the moment is gym equipment, as people try and create their own home exercise areas. This is how it is – home offices, home workouts, home living.

Naturally, such is the way my brain is now functioning, this gives me the idea for a video – to have Olive and Mabel signing up for membership of my newly created garage gym. Which is why I find myself this evening, on a walk with the dogs in the nearby woods, foraging for six sticks of different sizes, all for one brief visual joke in the sketch. Mabel does at least earn herself a credit as assistant to the props department by carrying one of the smaller sticks back to the car. Olive helps out in her own way by destroying a couple and I have to go and fetch more as I know the originals won't be seeing the light of day for another twenty-four hours or so. And even then they are going to be in no fit state to appear on screen.

Once I start filming, I realise that it's not going to go down as the dogs' greatest performance. They sit, concentrating very hard, as if they have begun reading about the Stanislavski method but it's not yet coming naturally to them and is rather wooden as a result. In fact, they are merely staring at two rubber balls that I am holding for the first half of the video. What's more, Olive ruins a couple of takes by choosing crucial moments to clean her backside, which she has been struggling with since eating some of the props on our walk. Eventually the actor-director-executive producer runs out of patience, so it will have to do.

For the final shot at the end, I manage to persuade Mabel to stand in a child's paddling pool which has cost me thirty pounds – all for about five seconds of screen time – and which I am unlikely ever to use again. Perhaps I could invite local children round to play in it, although I accept that this might not be the best way to introduce myself to the neighbourhood. To that cost you can add the ninety pounds for buying the online licence to some pumping bass gym music which, in the final video, you can barely hear.

My God, I suffer for my art.

Saturday 16 January

> '...and I to my office till very late, and my eyes began to fail me, and be in pain which I never felt

to now-a-days, which I impute to sitting up late writing and reading by candle-light.'

DIARY OF SAMUEL PEPYS, 19 January 1664

I'm currently looking to see if I can move house again. Caroline doesn't know, but I am wondering if there is any property for sale in the beautiful land of Watopia. Although I accept that the possibility is rather slim, since no such place exists.

The chances are that you have not even heard of Watopia, it being a fictional land of Zwift, an online exercise app which allows you to link a stationary bike and the power you produce on it, to an avatar of yourself. Other people in other countries are doing the same – putting on some very real Lycra wherever they might be, and all of our virtual representations then cycle happily – and in my case quite slowly – round very accurate replicas of cities and regions in our own world. Or through the fantastical landscapes of Watopia.

'But, Andrew...' you cry, 'that sounds like a load of nonsense.'

Well of course it is, but it is a very enjoyable nonsense. I admit I used to frown upon it as strongly as my eyebrows would allow, but the significant attraction of it at the moment is that it allows me to achieve the twin goals of punishing exercise while at the same time firmly turning my back on the real world.

Although I do recognise that this might not be the healthiest solution to the problems out there, I am nevertheless currently a strong advocate of burying my head in the sand. This is nothing to do with me discovering that some of my socks are out of a carefully arranged order, but just a case of trying to shut out the news and the negativity.

So today, as so often, I make the decision to head off into a world untainted by such problems. A meeting place where people from all corners of the globe come together to give you cheery encouragement and end sentences with just a bit too much lively punctuation. There you can find yourself cycling with or racing against somebody who might be in their flat in Tokyo, or a shed in Canada, or a cupboard under the stairs in the Czech Republic. I cycle along litter-free roads, past perfectly maintained buildings with strangers shouting 'Looking strong, bud!' or 'Nice work, my friend!!!!!' Yes, it's all a little bit odd, but never are people passing judgement or shouting opinions one way or another on all the vexing issues of the world. It's as if everybody has taken ecstasy and gone to Switzerland.

There is also a further aspect of human connection to it. I haven't seen my family for months but I can arrange to meet one of my brothers on Zwift – he pedalling away at night in his house in Troon, me in a garage in Cheshire with rain hammering against the window, yet both of us cruising down sunny Watopian desert roads.

And both of us perfectly recreating reality by cycling side by side for a couple of hours and not saying a single word to each other.

Of course, relentless positivity can eventually wear thin – and certainly lose its meaning. There is, in fact, all manner of cult-like exercise available, where you can lose yourself in a communal world of online sweat, endorphins and muscular, toned optimism. Often these collectives are led by the overexcited and evangelical. Glistening creatures with brilliant teeth and lustrous hair who regularly inform you that you are crushing it. In truth they don't really know if you are crushing it or not, as you may be crying, or eating crisps on the sofa having given up after three minutes. Or multitasking by crying while eating crisps. A terrible day cannot necessarily be remedied by some press-ups and group shouting – but whatever gets you through the night. I think we're all just trying to reassure each other that everything is OK.

At least these online shenanigans do involve some exercise. They are, though, largely for the desperate middle-aged who frequently thrash around in pools of sweat barely able to breathe, because we have to in an attempt to defy time and gravity. For youngsters, who would (probably wisely) wonder why on earth you would willingly expend such effort, it is interactive gaming that instead offers the connection which has been missing from all of our lives. Just as we chat on the phone or send texts and message online, they can ramble on about whatever they need to get off their chests, but do so while letting an animated collection of graphics expend the effort for them, maiming an enemy or possibly an associate by mistake. It is such a well-established way of existing for so many people that more mundane matters in the other plane are referred to – as things invariably are now – with an acronym: IRL, or 'In Real Life'.

The truth is that the world of online fantasy (I'm not sure why WOOF hasn't caught on) simply has an enormous appeal at the moment. It always has, but now even more so. With the real world appearing hostile and constricting, why would you not be drawn into a place where life is all about enjoyment, where you can cut loose and where your options seem to be without limit? Virtual reality has that overriding attraction of being a better – or at least more immediately fulfilling – plane of existence than the original. In one world you might have lost your job, or be struggling socially, or generally feel that you are failing. Here in WOOF you can be a king or queen.

And if we are honest, this kind of behaviour is not the sole preserve of teenagers reclining in bedrooms which are in dire need of a liberal spray of Febreze. We've all tended to this kind of behaviour over the past nine months – or certainly variations of it. While our physical world has become far smaller, the virtual world has been expanding and we spend so much of our lives on the internet – working, playing, or generally just messing about watching videos of dogs. We do whatever we can to fill the hours or to distract us from the unpleasantness.

The potential downside of all this time online has been well documented – the artificial world is so much more attractive to so many that the danger is of some sort of mental detachment or withdrawal from reality. And I know that Olive and Mabel partly exist in the virtual world themselves as an online escape. But while I am very fond of the fictional version, as I sit here stroking Olive's ears, or touching Mabel's nose to her great surprise, I know that IRL is where I would always choose to be.

Besides, I need to restrict my time online as I have also become aware of what appears to be a detrimental physical side-effect of our constant screen time. My eyes are getting worse. When I haven't been indulging in my other perfectly normal pastimes of cycling indoors or filming dogs, I have been catching up on a few box sets, and this evening it is another couple of episodes of *Gomorrah*, an outstanding Italian drama set among the Camorra mafia-type gangs of Naples. I know that it has been out for a few years now, but I hope that if I binge-watch it, I can pretend I was one of the early adopters and become one of those deeply tedious people who recommends something ad nauseum as the greatest piece of television ever made.

The key points of the narrative of most episodes (and I won't spoil it, because if you haven't seen it, you really should watch it – it's amazing) seem to be Italians shooting each other in the face. But the dialogue is very important to explain why a certain person has either shot or been shot in the face. And more and more I find myself squinting at the subtitles, before conceding defeat and moving to lie on the floor directly in front of the TV. Both Olive and Mabel watch me from the comfort of the sofas and then exhale in contented fashion as another Italian is shot in the face.

So I wonder if this decline in my eyesight is being caused by the amount of time I am currently spending looking at a phone or laptop. Our lives have become so dominated by these brightly flickering screens that when we emerge from them to focus on something else, we struggle. It seems to be a common ailment at the moment and I read a great deal about the harmful effects of 'blue light' and small font on luminescent screens. Which I, naturally enough, read about in small font on a luminescent screen.

Another online search – once more the irony does not escape me – advises that I should close my eyes for twenty seconds every now and again. And crucially, it also recommends that we take a moment to scan the horizon when we're outside.

And therein lies the problem. None of us has had the chance to scan a horizon for some time and I know that

I must do it soon or I am likely to go quite mad. But before I let that happen, I will make do with racing a Canadian man whom I'll never meet, up an imaginary volcano in my garage.

Thursday 21 January

A thick coating of snow has returned overnight. It was not entirely expected, so has that thrill of when you were young, going to bed in one world and opening the curtains in the morning to see that you have been transported to some new and enchanted place. My memory of childhood suggests that it snowed more often then, but this may just be one of the frequent lies that my memory tells. I am absolutely sure, though, that snow always seemed to arrive in this fashion – as a surprise gift, in a time when weather forecasters made their predictions with an air of great confidence masking a deeper uncertainty and in the end simply placed a variety of symbols around the map of the country to hedge their bets.

The new fall might not have quite same effect on me as it did a few decades ago, but still there is a hint of excitement, a flicker of what it once meant. And for the dogs, when the door opens, there is far more. Since arriving in our new home, we have had a fair few days of snow cover and both of them are possibly wondering how far we actually moved. Although in fact the presence of the snow means that they have little room for any thoughts other than the sensation which hits them, flying out into this magical scene and this most amazing day. Mabel spins and whirls around and around before beginning a series of high-speed laps of the garden, occasionally stopping to dig her snout into the cold layers of white. And then repeats the whole process. Every now and again she comes over to leap upon Olive, bat her in the face and encourage her to join in more fully, as senior dog is now taking it all in at a more leisurely pace, with a more seasoned eye and experienced nose.

But it is nice to see that Mabel, at least, will never lose her childish wonder.

Wednesday 27 January

I think it's 27 January. Or the 26th. A Friday I believe. Possibly Monday. It doesn't really matter as I am living the same day over and over – which would be fine if the day in question was when I learned to ride a bike or lost my virginity (not the same day), but instead it is merely a 24-hour session which passes like so many others. We get up and tick off the usual jobs and tasks at the usual times of the day. The hope is to somehow achieve those other little things that will make us feel normal and make us believe that we are moving forward. For now, it is the lack of variety which reminds us that we are not so much living as just getting through life.

I'm only glad that it's not the weekend – again, a feeling which might run contrary to popular opinion, but I always get the impression that we are making some sort of progress during the week. While the world is generally struggling to move, it does at least turn slowly from Monday to Friday – yes, grinding and squeaking as if about to topple off a rusty axis, but it is still moving. Yet at the weekend it comes to a shuddering halt and with the pause we all look around and notice all too clearly where we are. My mother describes every day as like Sunday at the moment – to which I respond that she sounds very similar to Morrissey, but since her points of musical reference stopped with early-period Kenny Rogers, I may be wasting my time. Which again, would be a significant help just now.

Besides, she's wrong – the working week is still just about clinging onto that description as people are doing whatever it is that everybody calls work now and therefore there is always the possibility of entertainment in the form of correspondence. As it is today when there is the novelty of an email arriving, inquiring about who owns the film rights to *Olive, Mabel & Me*. I start to type a reply that there is currently a very lively bidding war taking place between Universal and Warner Brothers. Pixar have also come in, but I confess that I'm uncertain about it going full animation. In the end I say none of this since it isn't true. Besides, I can't quite see the appeal of a film based on whatever flimsy Olive and Mabel story there is. It certainly doesn't have the strong emotional narrative that made something like

Marley and Me such a success. 'Man makes videos with his dogs and a lot of people watch them.' Pitch that to Spielberg and see how far you get.

So I am sure that nothing will come of it, but I do spend an idle hour or two wondering how it would work – probably with the story heavily dramatised and exaggerated to pull at the heart strings and with a couple of minor tweaks, such as Olive and Mabel being portrayed by poodle-based dogs. And perhaps my character being played by Paddy McGuinness.

Apart from that, there is little to report. This unvarying day ends, as they all do, lying on the sofa late at night watching television. And the rituals of this day, like any and every other, are completed by a familiar act involving one of our dogs, both of whom revel in habit and repetition. As I lie, Mabel pads over and sits in front of me, staring, before emitting the most pitiful questioning squeak – asking permission to board. A pat of the sofa is given to grant access and she hauls herself up, never jumps – initially missing the edge a couple of times with one of her back paws waving at thin air – before settling down behind my legs with her patented noise of satisfaction, a combination of groan, purr and sigh. Then she tucks herself into the crook of my knees and rests her head on my legs and I stroke her ears and tell her all is well, trying, I think, to convince myself far more than her. But if this is how it has to end, the coda to every day forever more, it's not a bad way to play out.

FEBRUARY 2021

Wednesday 3 February

Today I've been wondering how I would manage as a cowboy in Montana. I already suspect the answer is 'not well in the slightest', but this evening something has driven me to a real estate website dealing with property in that part of the world and I now peruse various ranches for sale.

I should make it clear that I have no intention of moving to Montana. Even if I did want to, I know that if I were to raise the idea over dinner quite a lively discussion would follow. It is just an idle reaction to that ongoing feeling of being hemmed in, living locally and travelling the same very short distance to the very same shops every few days.

I also marvel at the amount of land you can buy there for a relatively modest price. Here you would find the quiet, and here is somewhere you could scan a great deal of horizon. I'm willing to bet that those ranchers have outstanding eyesight.

I then take it further by considering how I might be

able to fund this life, bearing in mind that my ranching skills are minimal, so I look up the local broadcasting scene in the state capital, Helena.

Yes…yes…this could *work*, I think, as I start to put together the finer details. Every day I'll commute from our ranch, where Olive and Mabel have an untroubled run of 500 acres and yet still manage to get into next door's garden. After my two-hour drive down out of the mountains, I'll stop in at Diane's Bakehouse to pick up an oversized pastry and underachieving coffee, before heading to the local TV station. 'I don't know, Lindy…the traffic on that I-15 doesn't seem to get any better, but seeing you makes it all worthwhile!' I say to Lindy on reception (we have this kind of mildly flirtatious relationship). Gary the travel reporter strolls over and I josh with him about the roads, suggesting it must be his fault before we have a playful wrestle – although secretly I really do hate him, so put a bit more strength into the neck-hold than is strictly necessary. I then call up Bill Funkhouse Jr, the head coach of the Bobcats football team to find out if rumours are true that their quarterback has eloped with one of their wide receivers. Fortunately I've built up a strong rapport with Bill – we even had his family over to the ranch – and I get an exclusive interview which ends with him wishing both players well in their new life together. Years later, my tireless work and bribing of the selection panel pay off and I'm inducted into the Montana Broadcasters Hall of Fame with a gala ceremony in Conference Room 3 at the Marriott Airport Hotel, just outside Bozeman. I am slapped on the back and widely acclaimed – even mentioned by some in the same breath as legendary Montana broadcasters Lamont Wallis or Richard 'Shag' Miller. Sadly I have a few too many champagnes and, after an inappropriate comment to one of the attendees at a cement seminar in the next conference room, I am put into a cab.

Yes, indeed. I can see it all now.

After about an hour, I realise a couple of things – firstly, that I have taken pointless internet time-wasting to the next level, but also, more importantly, that I am suffering from *fernweh*. I don't realise it initially because I don't know the word but, as with a physical illness, all you have to do is type the symptoms into a search engine and the internet will provide a diagnosis which is twenty-three per cent accurate.

Fernweh is a sort of Wanderlust but, even more, it is a profound longing to be elsewhere with a literal translation of 'far-sore' or 'far-pain'. Curiously, Germans seem to have cornered the market in words of this ilk. It's true that they are a great travelling people, with a penchant for spreading their wings which, it must be said, has got them into a fair bit of bother in the past.

Throughout the last year and even more so in recent weeks, I have been thinking about other places. There have been offers from California and from Canada, from

South Africa and New Zealand. Offers to visit, offers to work, some serious, others not so. But most importantly every one of them is currently well beyond my reach.

Of course, we're all struck by this affliction. I know that Caroline is looking all the while to Australia and her brother and family over there. Her *fernweh* is equally severe, if not more so. I want to travel, whereas she needs to. But all we can do is watch from afar as those sunny Australian lives continue and appear largely untouched by the ills of the rest of the world. It does, though, come at a price – the country is hermetically sealed with an invisible wall beginning a few hundred yards out into the ocean. They live on and it looks and feels normal, but only as it once did to Jim Carrey in *The Truman Show*.

Are things made better or worse that we can see and hear across the great divide? That we can call upon almighty technology to bring us together even when far apart, to quote every mobile phone advertisement ever made? Yes, it helps in that we can talk so easily to exiled loved ones, but it does harm as well in teasing us with what we miss – showing us those other lives so clearly and so immediately that you feel you might be able to step through the screen. Yet while we are always looking, we are unable to touch. We can see but not feel what it is like to actually be there – we are Dorothy in the castle, trying to reach out to Auntie Em in the crystal ball, but with an unbreachable barrier between us. The other world is calling, but it is only light and glass.

Even without the disconnection from friends and family, there is that need to satisfy the in-built human desire to move. It has become painfully clear of late why we have always travelled as far and wide as our means of the time would allow. We do it to avoid the feeling of being trapped, of stagnating. And often driven by the unshakeable belief that things might be better elsewhere.

So the world stretches wider and our *fernweh* grows with it – distances greater and journeys unachievable, we look to other countries and we long for other lives.

But my pointless human contemplation is now being interrupted by two dogs, whose current longing is only for their bowls to be filled as it's precisely five o'clock and they are, in any case, quite certain that their whole world is here. Why would they need to look any further?

So I close the laptop on my wandering through Montana. Which of course isn't really Montana at all. It is just anywhere beyond the invisible barrier. All those places that we cannot reach now – everywhere we visit only in an idle dream.

Saturday 6 February

Often tedium can be a driving force. A motivation to do something. And sometimes it can even bring its own inspiration as I decide to make another video using the ennui of this month as its subject.

So I work out that Olive will have been doing lots of cookery. Baking perhaps…yes…and I make the necessary preparations by placing a few patches of flour on her head, while being very careful to keep it out of reach of her wandering and really quite massive tongue. Mabel, I imagine, has been working ineffectively on her music, so I persuade her, with no real difficulty, to clamber up onto one of the sofas and I bring in an enormous keyboard for her to perch behind.

Throughout the filming Olive performs admirably while Mabel for the first time appears genuinely baffled by what I am doing. As if something has clicked in her small, furry head and informed her that this is madness. She's right of course, but I persevere and, as I send it out there, it gets a nice reaction.

Meanwhile the older videos are still being passed on and observed around the world. A Japanese gentleman tweets out the bone video. His quote to accompany the film of Olive and Mabel is – justifiably – in Japanese. But a translation is offered just below, revealing a typically poetic Japanese description about the clip: 'It is like this when light for a moment pierces the gap and covers the darkness.'

I'd like to reply to him in Japanese and tell him that he has summed up perfectly what my dogs do for me just now.

Tuesday 9 February

There are several points throughout history where one could possibly say that we have peaked – Shakespeare or da Vinci, Michelangelo or Mozart, using language, brush strokes or notes to create works of such beauty and power that the world stops to look and listen, or simply marvel at what we can do. Yet today all those things may have been surpassed, as a lawyer in America takes part in an online hearing with a filter which presents him as a kitten.

I am very well aware that a Zoom meeting with animals involved has some potential. And here, the comedy of the absurd – often at play in Olive and Mabel videos – is made even better by the main protagonist being so desperate to escape the situation. His voice remains in the human tones and southern accent of the bewildered lawyer, but it is a kitten that looks around, ears down and with large, worried eyes darting from side to side, as it continues to talk, asking the judge about the possibility of proceeding with the case.

It may not stand the test of time quite in the same way as those masterpieces that have lifted us as a species throughout the centuries. But for now, the online world is united in joy as we watch this perfect work of art, over and over again.

'I'm not a cat,' suggests the lawyer-cat, helpfully.

Friday 12 February
What a beautiful day and a blessed release. I am able to travel for the first time in months as I drive north to Edinburgh to commentate on the match between

Scotland and Wales in the Six Nations, which is taking place tomorrow. It feels so strange but so liberating to be out, to be driving again on open and empty roads. To be going somewhere. To be *free*. I reflect on all of this as I sit in the back of the police car having been stopped for speeding on the M74.

Worse still is that as I hand over my licence, the officer in the driving seat recognises my name and, for about the first time in a year, it is not a dog-related association.

'Ah…heading up to do the game, are you?'

I nod, hoping that my combination of insincere smile and entry-level celebrity might save the day.

'Great stuff. Should be a cracker. What do you think about Darcy Graham starting on the wing?'

So I chat away, making the conversation that one does in such situations, imagining that a few seconds of casual banter is going to make the police chuckle and see you on your way with merely a warning to 'keep the speed down, you rascal' while ruffling your hair. Instead, he continues to write out the ticket.

'I have to say, you are by MILES my favourite commentator, so I really don't like doing this,' and he pulls a face and makes a slightly pained noise.

'Well then, isn't there something we can do about that?' I ask, winking, but immediately realise that this could be interpreted as offering him some sort of quick fumble in the bushes by the hard shoulder. In any case, the smiles and breezy chat have disappeared.

'Right, well, just mind how you go from now on.'

I notice as I leave the police car that there is a camera pointing to the back seat and I now fear, at some point in the future, appearing on one of those compilation TV programmes – perhaps a new one called *Awkward Celebrity Police Bribes* narrated by Danny Dyer.

Sunday 14 February

California, 1969 – the world's first successful electronic transmission is made, from one computer at UCLA to another at Stanford Research Institute.

Message – Test...test...

Message – Test passed! Good to connect! History!!

Message – Absolutely my friend. Say something else...

Message – OK...um...I think Governor Reagan is doing a great job.

Message – Christ, are you kidding?? You're a dick.

A message arrives today from a smiling, pleasant-looking woman on Instagram.

'You should be ashamed of yourself.'

This is undoubtedly true, I think. Although I also wonder about what, in particular. Perhaps she watched the game on Saturday. Or she's seen the police tape.

But it quickly becomes clear that it is dog-related,

---

* The first chat between the computers of UCLA and Stanford in October 1969 was not quite as described here. In reality, the system crashed two letters into their attempt to write 'login'. And so the historic first message transmitted between two computers was a simple 'lo'. Perhaps we should have left it at that.

as indeed most things are now. My second column in the *Sunday Times* is out and the lovely, kind Olive and Mabel utopia in which I have been living has been infiltrated. A land where people smile constantly, saying, 'Greetings…be well and happy, fellow dog person,' is now host to some unwelcome visitors.

This is the problem with becoming a columnist. People disagree with what you write and then feel compelled to tell you that you are wrong in quite a forthright manner.

I had been asked this month to give some pearls of wisdom for the country's many new dog owners, as it appears that a new law has been brought in whereby you have to own one. 'We really do feel that people like to have expert advice in a column,' said the editor who wasn't in any way dissuaded by my brilliant counterargument that I was not an expert. So I reluctantly agreed and decided simply to regurgitate some of the instructions we had read about when going through the puppy phase with Olive and Mabel.

'*Dog guru Andrew Cotter's essential tips…*' ran the strapline for the article which I was asked to retweet and which made me anxious. Firstly, in putting forward the notion that my advice is *essential* – as if without it your dog might simply expire. Secondly, offering the idea that I am somehow a canine guru, sitting crosslegged in a cave in the mountains, receiving vexed owners and telling them in a soft and wise voice how often they should treat their dog's anal glands. It's all asking for trouble, which has duly arrived.

I am rather stunned. This is Instagram after all, which is generally the most pleasant and positive of social media worlds (although I can't personally vouch for TikTok). It is where people offer a constant stream of hearts and LOLs and thumbs up and encouraging words. You know that there might not be genuine feeling behind all of them, but still your hunger to be praised or appreciated is fed. Just as when your mother might have told you a confusion of crayon lines was a work of art and deserved pride of place on the fridge. It still made you feel good, even if deep down you suspected it wasn't true. And what's more, that you should probably stop doodling and move out as you approached thirty.

So here on Instagram is the modern equivalent – where you can post a picture of a homemade cake and there will follow any number of comments to suggest that this is the finest cake produced in the long history of baked goods. It is where children and animals are unequivocally adorable and, even if we don't believe it, we tell each other they are because to those people who post them it's the truth. And isn't that what matters? Besides, to say that their child actually looks like a miniature version of Jocky Wilson would do nobody any good.

But it is somewhat jarring to see another side of things. I accept that I have been spoiled over the past months, receiving almost endless loveliness and kind words, but here is a slap to wake me from the Olive and Mabel dream. Of course, this is being massively over-sensitive at one person telling you that you should be ashamed. With another ordering me to 'stick to sport'. And OK, perhaps a few more telling me that I'm essen-tially clueless. But in the grand scheme of things, it surely doesn't really matter – this is gentle social media reaction compared to the constant streams of abuse which are received by some people.

And yet I feel strange. Deflated. And tired. At the moment it takes only a small thing to tip the mental balance and you are suddenly aware what a fine line you have been treading – believing that all is well when in fact you have for a long time been tiptoeing gently on brittle ground. All it can take is the slightest knock – some minor incident at the shops, in your car, at work. Or a stranger telling you that you should be feeling deep shame for puppy-raising advice. And you can fall.

I'm not really getting down about a couple of negative messages. It's something more than that, something big-ger underneath the surface – but a surface thin enough to be scratched away by only a sharp word or two.

The best thing to do, if you are living in a more frag-ile mental state than you perhaps realise – as many of us will be just now – would be to try and control what you see or hear, because it doesn't take much noise from outside to affect you, to trigger something. And yet how difficult that is when all the time we are drawn into the extremely noisy, out of control, trigger-happy world of the internet and social media.

The chattering feed is constant and to avoid it requires you to be either somebody with a modicum of willpower or simply a Luddite. And the latter would be my only option. Ah, to be a happy Luddite, steadfastly refusing to use the mechanics of the modern world. If social media had not come along, I could ingest my news and opinions in more manageable doses. And I suppose that I could still try to do that, with just a newspaper in the morning and perhaps an evening bulletin. Not quite such a full-on assault on the senses and sensitivities – everything done at a more leisurely pace. Like those early nineteenth-century weavers, happy in their work, taking three and a half days to make a small blanket.

But to imagine a world without social media now is to think of times before air travel or cars or television. That horse has well and truly bolted from the stable – he's probably over there telling the cow and the pig why they're wrong.

Because this is how we operate on social media, firmly setting up on one side or the other. Nuance is lost and there is nothing in between. There is no room here for the person who says, 'I'd really rather get all the facts before I make a judgement.' What's more, you never see the millions who, if forced, might only comment, 'I have no obvious opinion about your stance on politics, religion or dog husbandry.'

When given a platform, though, people will quickly decide that you must use it to say something. So many of those who are here have jumped in to pile on and shout and shame, hurling love in one direction and outrage another. Because it's a natural thing for humans to want: to *need* to make ourselves heard, to feel that we matter. And also, because it's become so quick and simple to do, while at the same time never easier to disregard the impact it can have.

Besides, in the wider realm of the internet, it seems that any reaction – good or bad – is desired. Because whichever one you have, it's interaction and that is the shining currency of the online world. The all-important traffic. But sometimes the very best thing to do is switch it off and shut it down. Go for a walk or perhaps read a decidedly unopinionated book. Better still, do as I do this evening and watch a terrible film while stroking the soothing head of a Labrador, filled with very few opinions except a total certainty that they are fond of you.

Technology though is not yet done with me as, late at night, an email comes in from the editor of the magazine.

'The good news is that it's the most clicked-on item across the whole paper. And the reaction is mostly positive!'

So I send the dogs to their beds and head upstairs myself. Mostly happy.

At least I think I am.

Tuesday 16 February

We are becalmed in the doldrums. Drifting along and no more than that. Technically the shortest month, this February already feels as if it has lasted for approximately a year and a half. Meanwhile, our days continue to be a most curious blend of the decidedly strange and the exceedingly mundane.

Firstly, the strangeness which is of course the general world situation, but there is also the additional, more specific oddness brought on by the characters of Olive and Mabel, most notable today in an approach from somebody asking if I had considered developing an Olive and Mabel wine. My immediate confession is that no, I had not considered this.

There have, as previously mentioned, been plenty of offers to use the dogs to sell merchandise which I might understand or even expect, once their popularity became clear – mugs, T-shirts, toys, calendars. But I freely admit that an Olive and Mabel wine has taken me somewhat by surprise.

While not an expert in either wine or marketing, it doesn't strike me that seeing two Labradors on a label would compel anyone to buy a bottle of Sauvignon Blanc. A damp dog aroma is not necessarily what you are looking for in the nose of a wine, or indeed the thought that the grape-trampling stage of the process might have been performed by a whole crew of industrious strays from the villages near the vineyard.

But then it is explained to me that it would be a fairly high-end wine, carefully selected from an established house and simply given our name. I am shown the look of a possible label and it almost sways me – there is a curious elegance to it and I think about a dog lover searching for something slightly different when perusing the shelves of their supermarket or off-licence and going for a bottle of smooth Olive red or immature Mabel white.

Once more though, the thing which stops me is the idea of somehow selling out – taking Olive and Mabel away from their world of innocence and fun and using them to flog stuff. Again, perhaps I am being too narrow-minded – after all, I grew up in a world of merchandised items featuring any number of favourites from popular culture such as Garfield, Charlie Brown or the Muppets and it didn't affect my enjoyment of the books, cartoons or television series. Although I may well have changed my mind if I had seen somebody staggering along the street, swigging from a bottle of Snoopy vodka.

But I still say no to it for the moment – and file it away in the folder of unusual offers, which now spills over.

Amidst all this oddness, where does our grounding come from? Inevitably it comes from those two creatures who are at the heart of the madness but are themselves masters of the mundane. One of the real strengths of Olive and Mabel, apart from their apparent marketability, is that they are a constant – a reassuring stability just when we need it more than ever.

Human lives might have changed beyond all comprehension, but those of dogs remain largely the same; even though their sphere of understanding is far smaller, they remain well within it, lives still revolving around the canine Holy Trinity of walking, eating and sleeping.

Olive and Mabel have no idea about the strange offers that come our way on their behalf. And, unlike us, they have no need of any virtual, fantasy world of escape; for the most part they appear to be very satisfied with reality as long as it has a decent selection of sofas.

Olive in particular firmly believes that soft furnishings are where she belongs – this is her chosen domain. Having said that, she does still ask our permission most of the time but has recently developed the deeply frustrating habit of remaining on the floor even once we have tapped the sofa and said, 'Come on then.' It's as if she wants us to thoroughly demean ourselves by begging. Which we assure each other that we will never do.

A few minutes later and she is still standing there – either uttering the most pathetic whimper or even resting her head on the sofa and staring up at us, conveying the great sadness in her life. And we are reduced to pleading with her to jump up. We are unsure whether it is because she doesn't understand or because she is aware of her new-found fame and is being annoying. Very possibly the latter.

Mabel spends the vast majority of her day wandering around carrying something and seemingly fretting about the state of the world – the positive sign is that she does so with her tail in perpetual motion as if convincing herself that actually everything is fine. Then she knocks something off a table with it and starts to worry a bit about that as well. Quite often that tail is smacking Olive in the face, which she seems to bear with considerable sufferance and good humour as an occupational hazard of dog life, before taking herself off to bed.

They are not the most taxing days for the dogs, but they seem quite content. And in their contentment with the simple things, we find a bit of it ourselves. Although a little bit more stimulation wouldn't go amiss for both them and us.

Or perhaps we could just have half a glass of the *Olive and Mabel 94*. Which I'm told has quite a lively bouquet.

Thursday 18 February

TO-DO LIST *
1. *Go for run (with dogs)*
2. *Cycle*
3. *Walk dogs*
4. *Buy food*
5. *Eat*

* *Applicable to all days until further notice.*

I have barely the energy to type. This is entirely down to my tried and tested technique for dealing with everything that is currently going on – constant exercise to the point of exhaustion.

If it doesn't sound like the most sensible plan then that's because it very possibly isn't, but the results are addictive. It numbs the sensations – silences all the noise of the world. You make yourself so tired that you can't get overstressed at anything. You can barely move in the evening either, but that is one of the side-effects listed in very small print on my homemade medication, which I choose to ignore.

Another major drawback is that it is far from ideal to attempt this in a middle-aged man's body, although in that I have little choice. Yes, I know that something is likely to tweak or snap or possibly even fall off and then what will I do? But I ignore any potential repercussions further down the line. Besides, I can't seem to ease up – I am determined to tackle the darkness with a potent combination of endorphin release and massive fatigue.

I am well aware that rest days are important – even more so as we get older – yet every day I indulge in some sort of training and very often a run where I try to combine my own goals with obligations for dog exercise. Mabel, full of the energy and idiocy of youth, is all for three heavy sessions a day, with possibly some weights in the evening. Olive more often looks as if she is considering that a rest day might be wise – why don't we all just recover on the sofa together? Or perhaps ingest vital restorative proteins in the form of chicken scraps?

Another reason that there is a categorical imperative for exercise is that I now exist in a near constant state of snacking. Different mealtimes have lost their clearly defined status and merge into one never-ending performance as I graze throughout the day like a cow. This is partly caused by a need to get up and do something to break up the monotony, but also doubtless due to being in close proximity to a fridge. And so I steadily empty both it and nearby cupboards, going through them all as if auditioning for the title role in *The Tiger Who Came to Tea*.

I really do feel for my dogs in having to witness this behaviour. Olive, in particular, wishes that she had such freedom and frequently she will make a similar trip, returning to her bowl outside regulation feeding times to push it around the floor with noisy metal clangs, first licking and then just staring into its depths as if something new might suddenly materialise. Quite often I reach the same point by late afternoon when I have exhausted all other options and am gazing into the fridge hoping that something fabulous might appear, but left with only an old bowl of pasta and a blueberry yoghurt, am wondering if I might create some new outlier in fusion cuisine.

Nothing, though, can stop me eating and eating, pausing only to drink no end of tea and coffee then eat some more. I reach the point where I half expect to feature in the televised governmental briefings – the special scientific adviser of the day requesting that we move on to the next slide, which shows an inexorably upward-moving graph of my calorific intake. 'We have to be honest here and admit that this is a worrying development,' they say, before opening it up to questions.

Yet no matter how much I eat, I know it is still far more the mental than the physical need which compels me to pull on trainers or Lycra. And it seems that I am well supported by the multitudes who are being swept up in exercise mania. Gyms are still closed and all organised sporting activities forbidden, so people are doing whatever they can. Wherever you look there are those of all shapes and sizes trudging down trails or skipping along pavements. It used to be that anybody you saw out running was fairly serious about it. Now, huge sections of the population appear to be in a state of transit, many with the look of those who are putting themselves through real discomfort because they know they have to. Shuffling along with a pained or haunted expression, running with no obvious destination in mind. Running to keep going, running to feel better. Just running to avoid standing still.

Which is how it is with us. Or one of us, anyway. So I temporarily interrupt my snacking, put collars around necks and head into the woods nearby. Just a walk tonight though, as we have already done our major therapeutic exercise, out early this morning on a pre-dawn trip to the beach. There we started by the light of a head torch and with every step taken the sun crept up from behind the dunes. The tide was low and the waves a far off, gentle sound as we three ran and ran – all happy just for that time at least, bounding along together on the firm sand.

Although as ever, Mabel did occasionally look round anxiously, wondering what might be after us.

I know for certain what's chasing me.

Friday 19 February

Today, the United States has landed another rover on Mars and there is something about the news which is cheering. Of course, it doesn't immediately affect us but as we continue to get into a bit of a mess here on Earth, it's nice to see that we are still achieving as a species. 'Perseverance' has touched down and will now wander about doing very important things while also releasing a small drone helicopter called 'Ingenuity'.

This isn't the first man-made object to land on Mars – far from it. That honour goes to the Soviet Union who, as early as 1971, managed to land their snappily titled 'Mars 2' probe on the planet – 'land' being a very generous description of it hurtling into the surface at a high rate of knots. Since then, a number of missions have reached the Red Planet in a rather more controlled fashion. Of those, the 2012 visitor 'Curiosity' is still active and now has company.

I notice, Russian names apart, that they all bear titles which sum up the best traits of human beings and I'm glad there are people among us who still have that inquisitive nature, in addition to the combination of genius and optimism, which will carry us forward. I confess that my own personality would be more likely to launch a series of missions called *Unlikely to Succeed* or *Fingers Crossed 1* and *2*, but it is encouraging just to see, as we surround ourselves with examples of human ineptitude, that we are still capable of wondrous things. Even at the very closest point in Mars' elliptical journey round the sun, it is almost forty million miles from Earth. Yet as I look at the pictures coming back, so clear as if they are simply images of a desert in Arizona, I admire the *fernweh* of the human race which takes it ever further out into the universe. And at the same time ponder the fact that I can't travel twenty miles to cross the border into Wales.

Wednesday 24 February

Today we made it to eleven. Eleven dog food brands have now approached us to see if Olive and Mabel might be interested in working with them. Well, I can confidently state that Olive would certainly be interested but, as with all those that have come before, I turn this one down. If Olive knew the response that I was writing it would probably tip her over the edge and she would savage her hitherto beloved owner and thereafter try to fashion her own reply. The PR representative of the dog food in question would then receive an email simply saying 'YaS Plezz fodd'.

Yes, I might have recently agreed to provide a voiceover for a dog food commercial (mostly to pay for an almost constant purchasing of dog food), but I'm still determined not to associate the dogs themselves with any product – tasty treats, natural, grain-free food or otherwise.

One of the most common types of enquiry I receive gives an insight into the incredibly simple way advertising can work on social media – and offers a path to a career which any number of youngsters seems to consider the dream job: 'Influencer'.

It is one of the words of our times. The title alone hints at something powerful – the job itself appears glamorous and would seem to involve earning money without having to put in a huge amount of work. Why wouldn't it appeal to any teenager?

Emails rattle in from PR companies – often based in the up-and-coming areas of London and usually with go-getting, energetic names like Spank or Jazzle. The missive invariably includes an emoji which lets you know that the go-getting Spank or Jazzle are employing go-getting twenty-somethings because they throw emojis around like full stops – and often one which has no discernible relevance to the actual request. Of course, it will all become perfectly standard in years to come. A funeral parlour sending out an email saying they are sorry for your loss, accompanied by a sad face. Or with the unfortunate typo of a flamenco dancer. Or an aubergine.

Anyway, once every week or so comes an emoji-laden question asking Caroline, 'How much would your client charge per x number of posts on Instagram? (Blushing face.)'

Today we did feel like sending one back saying, 'Twelve million pounds (flexing bicep)' because I have no interest in doing it but, well, you never know.

So established is the profession now that there are even recognised tiers of influencers as the class society is alive and kicking on social media. The levels are based on the number of followers you have on your account and on Insta (as the kids, or anybody under forty, calls it) they are loosely as follows:

(i) Nano-influencer
Between 1,000 and 10,000 followers. This qualifies you to get a few dollars for posting a photo in which you are putting on a certain type of make-up. Or wearing a particular pair of trainers or a hat. The fee might even be just the hat.

(ii) Micro-influencer
Between 10,000 and 100,000 followers. Somebody who might also post photos of themselves wearing

trainers or a hat, but will receive up to $1,000 for doing so. Plus the hat thrown in for good measure.

(iii) Mid-tier influencer
From 100,000 to one million. This is where we find Olive and Mabel, wearing neither make-up, trainers or hats. Nor eating any type of food in a video with me chuckling and saying, 'Hahaha... WOW... You sure like that food, girls!' Apart from anything else, they are Labradors and so the endorsement of them eating a foodstuff carries zero weight.

Above and beyond this we are into the realms of the faintly ridiculous.

(iv) Macro-influencer
Five hundred thousand to one million followers. The chances are very high that this is somebody you still haven't heard of. It might be a big player but somebody who has made their name on social media – incubated and raised entirely within the Instagram world. They post therefore they are, and they will spend an inordinate amount of time delivering pictures which all look the same. But you can see the reasoning. They could expect up to $10,000 to say they use a cleaning product, even if they quite obviously don't use it. Their cleaning product is whatever their cleaner brings with them because

they're too busy working on the pose and setting up their lighting.

And finally...

(v) Mega-influencer
Over one million followers. This is more likely to be a major star – somebody who has made their name in some other field such as film or music – social media is an additional thought. Almost certainly the additional thought of an agent. But if they are waiting for the next big acting role or working on the next album and want to earn $50,000 for a photo where they put on some nail polish, I say why not?

Although I do wonder what the return is for this kind of investment. The bigger the name, the more obvious it is that they are not really fans of the product. If they haven't cropped the picture properly you might even see the giant bag of cash being handed over.

It is also curious to see the other type of value we have placed on the number of followers somebody might have on social media. Not just the actual cold, hard monetary value but the way that person is viewed – the status accorded to them. We are conflating 'Is this person important?' with 'How many followers do they have?' Apparently the request which most often comes the way of anybody who works for Twitter or

Instagram is 'Can you get me verified? Can you get me a blue tick?' as if that gives them a validation which they didn't have before.

Yet it clearly matters – many are the people who have gone so far as to buy followers. In the past you could pay for as many fake disciples as you wanted, although much of this practice was shut down after an investigation by the *New York Times* in 2018. A company based in a tiny office above a restaurant in Florida was found to be the source of thousands of bot accounts which then marched in bot-like fashion out onto the internet and artificially inflated the following and importance of any number of people. Subsequently those people might have started to believe their own importance as well.

I am only glad I'm not a teenager again with social media so dominant – going through a stage of life which is awkward and insecure enough, where you already feel that pressure to be popular and are now hoping to receive lots of likes, or perhaps wondering why you don't have quite as many follower requests as others. If Orwell is right and the picture of the future is a boot stamping on a human face forever, then it is only if taken as a selfie, to be posted with the words 'So, *this* happened' and a thumbs-down emoji, plus the hashtag #ouch. Or as a meme with the accompanying text 'MONDAY VIBES'.

In so many ways I have tried to make Olive and Mabel

an escape from the nonsense of the human world. It just happens that they have made their names in one of the most ridiculous parts of it. Although perhaps man and beast are not so different. After all, Mabel demands likes constantly. And Olive still very much wants to be a dog food mega-influencer.

MARCH 2021

Monday 1 March

'The horrible thing about the Two Minutes Hate was not that one was obliged to act a part, but that it was impossible to avoid joining in...

...And yet the rage that one felt was an abstract, undirected emotion which could be switched from one object to another like the flame of a blowlamp.'

GEORGE ORWELL, 1984

March.

Springtime...the seasons change and a new year is about to begin.

That's right, a new year. You see, I have an alternative idea of when to mark the turning of a year and am no longer bound by the idea of celebrating it on the first of January. In this regard I have become like China, or

Zoroastrians, or perhaps even a Zoroastrian on a work placement in China. But it is my devotion to the church of Olive and Mabel which means that I now think in different terms and we are fast approaching the time when it all began – the mass cancellation of sporting events which would eventually lead to me turning to them both and saying, 'Right then, let's see if we can make you two into global celebrities.'

This weekend, the progress we have made in year one of the Labradorian calendar seems uncertain, since the match that I should have been working on yesterday – France versus Scotland – has been postponed owing to a Covid outbreak in the French camp. In news which we suspect is not entirely unrelated, about a third of the French squad was spotted the week before, playing fast and loose with the current guidelines by gathering in an Italian waffle house. There is undoubtedly a certain laissez-faire French attitude involved here – if only they had a phrase for it. I like to think that they were all celebrating a year of Olive and Mabel, but in reality they probably just wanted to have some waffles.

But now, such is the way of things, comes the backlash. It makes people angry that they could have done something so stupid – this, at least, is very much more in keeping with the current guidelines of everything making everybody angry.

We shouldn't be taken aback that rage is a default emotion for many right now; after all, the circumstances of the past year are not conducive to relaxation and contentment. In this I am far from exempt, feeling constantly snappy and irritable, although those who know me would point out that this is not a major lifestyle change. But take even the jollier creatures in the world and watch them turn when denied those things which they love. I know only too well the death stare of Olive and Mabel when food is not forthcoming. And I'm sure there will be behavioural scientists somewhere with demonstrable proof of this, having carried out experiments whereby rats in a laboratory were deprived of their usual manner of existence and within days began openly fighting with each other, or scurrying off to a corner to tap away on miniature laptops, issuing all manner of abuse under the pseudonym @ratboy97.

Because, of course, the turbulent, foaming sea of unpleasantness where the anger really manifests itself is social media. Here, the collective can have their two minutes of hate and perhaps more, working themselves into a frenzy at the target of their loathing, only now on a million different screens.

What it is that agitates them doesn't really matter. Certainly there are no end of subjects on which to turn the scorching blowlamp, with the pandemic not only creating the general feeling of tension but adding new material about which we can rail and, what's more, setting us neatly into distinct camps with opposing viewpoints.

Even without the more extreme opinions and

conspiracy theories, there are seemingly intelligent people who will have a different thought to the central advice on how things should be dealt with. No masks, no vaccine. I am only struck by the fact that there appear to be people who neither want lockdown nor seem to want the only way out which is being offered.

As usual, I will turn to Olive and Mabel for something of a salutary tale. Let me call it 'The Fable of the Stubborn and Imbecilic Dog'.

A man one day was out for a walk with his dogs, when these three happy creatures discovered that their usual gate on the other side of a field was tied shut. Not wishing to abandon the walk and have his dogs stare at him all afternoon in a fashion most irksome, the man clambered over and moved down the hedge on the other side, thereby to find a gap through which they all could pass. One duly located, it was as simple as tapping at the ground and summoning the blessed hounds to follow him to the other side. The younger, light-coloured dog happily did so, but even upon seeing that it was possible, the older, dark one resolutely stood and stared, steadfastly waiting for the locked gate to be opened so that she might exit by her chosen means even though t'was now impossible. This made the man sore with rage, but the dog would not be moved.

Now, although a hugely irritating and true event from a couple of weeks ago, it doesn't really work as a parable unless I embellish it with a bull in the field charging towards Olive and threatening to do her untold harm. As it is she was quite happy in there eating grass and would probably still be there now if I hadn't climbed back in there and shoved her towards the gap in the hedge.

But anyway, disagreement over what seem to be matters of common sense means that vaccines, masks and social distancing are added to the list of things not to discuss with friends if you want to maintain that status: 1) Politics 2) Religion 3) Epidemiology and the treatment of viral pandemics.

The situation is so divisive, where friends or family might find themselves on opposing sides. Add to all of this the already difficult domestic situations – everybody trapped together in houses with daily concerns about work and few enjoyable pastimes or activities to divert us – and it is no surprise that there is simmering discontent. I have little doubt that those who fire off expletive-laden rants are not only angry at their targets but at things far closer to them. As much as there is a human need to love, there seems to be the need to hate as well. There is certainly that fundamental need to make oneself heard and to feel that you matter.

So here we are – reaching the stage where a good many people are leaving social media. Quite often it's celebrities who announce the news that they are leaving through a post on social media.

The alternative is that you stay there but try to counteract it all by posting something which will provide light, comical, dog-based relief – as if the face of the enemy in 1984 had been briefly interrupted by a vignette of Winston Smith's basset hound tripping over its ears. This evening an email arrives from somebody whose fiancée has been suffering from anxiety. Grandparents had been lost and family relationships broken down in recent months. Working as a teacher only added to the stress, but a dog video now and again had helped.

This is when I am reminded of the rather more important side of Olive and Mabel, so it encourages me to keep on putting them out, if they help in any way with positivity. Yes, they are deeply silly videos, but sometimes deep silliness is what we need. And what dogs will so often manage to provide. Two minutes of watching Olive and Mabel doing very little is always going to be better than two minutes of hate.

'...*this disease making us more cruel to one another than if we are dogs,*' wrote Samuel Pepys in 1665, with London firmly in the grip of the plague, and sounding every inch the cat lover he was. But we know the truth. Dogs will help us through it all as a loving antidote to the hate.

Although I do accept that chihuahuas can be very angry indeed.

Thursday 11 March
We have fallen into the habit of three walks a day, sometimes four.

The benefits for all concerned are obvious. For Olive and Mabel a walk means everything – or at least everything that is not food-related (Olive) or physical contact-related (Mabel). I have been told that beyond edibles the very best thing you can give your dog is a bit of freedom. The chance to sniff the air and examine any amount of indeterminate brown matter is really very important to them.

It is why Mabel in particular shows such excitement at the prospect, spinning around with her mouth opening and closing, the point of which is not immediately apparent. Olive is far more loath to lose her inhibitions but her raised ears and jaunty stride still give the game away.

For people too, it is invaluable. It is a chance to let off steam, chatting away to our small companions, who look up occasionally as if giving the impression of listening, but are largely lost in their own thoughts and concerns – in which it is not unlike many human conversations.

But whether they are paying attention or not, I do enjoy a stroll, and with these two it is, for the most part, a relaxing affair where you can hear the birdsong and take in the world. How different it must be if you are the keeper of one of those more talkative dogs. Quite often we will hear the forest echoing to that shrill sound – a repetitive bark which makes your ears bleed and sets off car alarms half a mile away, with their constant shouted requests to, 'Pay attention to me and THROW

THE FUCKING TENNIS BALL.' And I give a prayer of thanks that Olive and Mabel express their excitement and desires more through a silent dance and intense stare than anything else.

I am also grateful when I compare their walking abilities to those of Mungo, my mother's bullmastiff, who I have occasionally had the misfortune to walk in Troon. I say misfortune only because he quite often decides to simply give up midway through an outing and lie down on the ground where he can have a think about things. He will eventually get moving again but this often takes about three or four days of steady persuasion, by which time a crowd of helpful townsfolk have come down to douse him with pails of water before an attempt to refloat at high tide.

Above all, though, I enjoy walking our dogs because it is real and it is simple – the alternative to an increasingly surreal and complicated human world.

Take, for example, the most curious news item of the day. Tucked away, a few pages apart from the very weightiest headlines, is a report that an NFT by Beeple has been sold by Christie's for $69 million. Now, there is a good chance that many parts of that sentence make no sense to you at all and that you are now merely giving a polite nod, as I did for large chunks of *Mastermind* or as Olive did when I expounded on why she shouldn't be dancing with cattle. But I will do my very best here to explain.

Let us firstly examine the easiest part of it, in that Beeple is the pseudonym of an artist whose actual name is Mike Winkleman and his particular field of expertise is digital art. Next, an NFT is a 'non-fungible token' – fungible meaning entirely interchangeable. Therefore, if something is non-fungible it is deemed to be unique. If you are still with me, that unique thing can also be purchased with the proof of ownership stored on a digital ledger called a blockchain. This digital recording is essentially how crypto-currency works and it's how somebody has paid almost 70 million dollars for Beeple's artwork called *Everydays – the first 5,000 days* which is a collage of images created by him, with one made every day since he started the process in 2007.

Naturally, this being the way of things, the digital artwork was bought in an online auction using digital currency. And the full-resolution artwork is now going to be displayed in a virtual museum.

Practically everything connected with this story is not only non-fungible, but non-tangible.

The reason I bring up this very modern tale is that it does show how much we are taking our lives into the virtual world, but it's also worth noting that Beeple has created something which is a sort of diary – it is as much a daily chronicle of our times as Pepys' diary was of his. And in fact, Beeple's very pricey masterpiece has out-lasted Pepys' decade of effort by three years – each and every day since he began, recorded in an extraordinary piece of art. I'm not saying it's worth $69 million, but a round of applause at least.

I do now wonder if I could bring together a collage of the Olive and Mabel videos which were released online – special and unique and therefore unable to be funged, selling at Christie's with a reserve price of five dollars. But in the end I give up trying to comprehend it all, so instead I grab the leads, Mabel starts her dance again and I take them out for a healthy dose of reality, struck once more by the thought that human beings are incredible – capable of the levels of ingenuity that can create such wonders. Using the full depths of our imagination and intelligence to fashion these artificial planes where commodities – and perhaps we – will all exist in the future.

I'm also struck by the thought that Beeple would be quite a good name for a dog.

Friday 12 March

The high point of the day is having a new dishwasher delivered. Ordinarily I'm not sure that this should pass the quality control test to make the pages of a diary but, such is the state of affairs, it now seems to qualify as one of the biggest events in the social calendar. The need for its arrival is pressing as the original is in an advanced stage of senility and now forgets what its role in life is, doing no more than shifting food debris from one plate to another. But as the two workmen arrive to install it, we realise that this is the most company we have entertained indoors for about a year.

Their presence also reminds me just how useless Olive and Mabel – and possibly all Labradors – are as guard dogs. Olive does initially bark but it is only a happy exclamation and she quickly moves on to greeting anybody who has arrived as the friend for whom she has been waiting her whole life. Mabel is more wary, but can be very easily won over with the slightest touch and, what's more, remains entirely silent throughout the whole episode. Any burglar could be wheeling objects out to a van and Mabel would be a hindrance only by getting in the way and looking a little bit nervous. Olive would be offering encouragement and good wishes for further thieving ventures. But again, their presence is better than nothing. And a cat would very probably have been the insider who made the call to let an intruder know when the owners were out and where the most valuable stuff was to be found.

Monday 15 March

Today I prepare for an online awards ceremony, having been put forward in the category of 2020 Sports Commentator of the Year. I had suggested that I didn't really want to be nominated, for what I felt was the very valid reason of practically no sport having taken place in 2020. This didn't seem to dissuade the BBC, who suggested that my dog-based commentaries might sway the judging panel and besides, it would be impolite to turn them down. I agreed but spent this morning practising my magnanimous face. An awards ceremony by Zoom is clearly where human beings have become as absurd as it's possible for a species to be. It certainly has potential to be more tortuous than a standard ceremony, although it does offer the opportunity to switch off your screen and blame connection issues while you smash up your room in weeping rage, swearing at the injustice of it all, before realising you haven't muted your microphone and all the judges have heard what you think of their parentage. I have contemplated dressing up in full evening wear for comic effect, but settle on a shirt and tie for the first time in months. I then wonder why I haven't been emailed a link to connect and, after further enquiries, am told that there is no actual ceremony, online or otherwise.

As it happens, I go down as one of the unmentioned in the category and now sit, smartly dressed, eating my dinner in front of the television. I feel that I might as well use my well-rehearsed generous/magnanimous face, so I applaud as Olive hops up onto the sofa, leaning over to Mabel and whispering through a forced smile, 'Great...well done her. *Absolutely* deserves it.'

Wednesday 24 March

I have been reminded today on Twitter that I really should put out another Olive and Mabel video. In truth I could write this in any page of the diary since it is a daily occurrence. It is obviously a very nice thing to read since it demonstrates quite clearly that people like the videos, but I am also well aware now that six weeks and more have passed since I last pressed send on anything of note, which is the longest gap since I first unwittingly began the Olive and Mabel adventure almost exactly a year ago.

I do have genuine excuses, with life and other work getting in the way, and in an ideal world the ideas would come easily. But they don't. Or the idea arrives but is not followed shortly after by a successful filming – usually because it proves impossible as the dogs behave like dogs, rather than classically trained actors who graduated from RADA followed by several years honing their skills in provincial theatre.

Fortunately I do have another idea to try out today, whereby I am playing cards with Olive and Mabel, but in terms of production it has so far proved one of the most labour intensive. Apart from anything else I have had to buy all of the props required, since rifling through every cupboard only confirmed my suspicions that we own neither poker chips, a green baize table covering, nor – strangely – a set of Dinosaur Top Trumps. And if you want to buy all of those things at the moment, there is only one place available. So with hundreds of millions of others, off I head to Amazon.

It is perhaps the one company which best sums up the modern world – the behemoth which we keep on feeding through our appetite for things. Cheap things, immediate things. The balance was already tipping heavily in its favour before the pandemic and now, with fewer and fewer alternative choices during lockdown days, it has become an elephant sitting on one side of the scales. Which sounds rather like the kind of random item it offers me based on my browsing history: I have befuddled a tiny corner of the Amazon brain, confusing the algorithm. So varied and odd is my shopping selection that under the line 'Based on your recent purchases' it looks as confused as I do when pondering what to get a nephew or niece for Christmas, before settling on cold, hard cash. Here, with that option unavailable, Uncle Amazon throws its questioning hands up in exasperation, then tentatively suggests a mixture of children's toys, gambling items and books by Ben Fogle. And, what's more, I could have them delivered by tomorrow. Or this afternoon. Or yesterday. Even as I click, they will be getting picked up from a dark corner of one of the enormous warehouses which the company insists on calling 'fulfilment centres'. They are then whisked around the country on the lorries, possibly soon to be rebranded 'dream transporters'.

I know it is not healthy for one business to so dominate the market. Or every market. I am also sure that our devotion to quickly bought and easily perishable goods is probably not an environmentally happy path to follow into the future. But I also don't know what the answer is to change it, beyond entirely altering the psychological make-up of humans. And realistically I haven't got time to do that. Besides, I am perhaps compromised now in my judgement, since one of the limbs of this many-armed consumer god has provided work for me as a commentator – or, as I think we are properly titled, 'word weavers'. So I will simply try and do as much purchasing as I can from smaller, independent businesses. Or perhaps – even more simply – purchase less.

Anyway, the props having duly arrived, I get on with the task of preparing the set and I wonder what people might think if they could see the lengths to which I go for this short dog-based sketch. As it happens, I soon receive my answer. Caroline comes into the room to see me laying out poker chips on a layer of green baize and gluing some standard playing cards to the newly bought deck of Dinosaur Top Trumps. She sighs in weary resignation and turns immediately round again.

A short while later, the video goes out and messages very swiftly inform me that people are delighted to see Olive and Mabel returning to their screens.

'YES…Olive and Mabel are BACK…'

'Love it! NEED MORE OF THESE!!'

Because the demand of the consumer is never-ending.

Friday 26 March
Something curious happens in the car today as I find myself sobbing while listening to classic eighties hit 'I've

Got You' by Split Enz. Most odd. It is a fine song with a refrain suggesting that 'I don't know why sometimes I get frightened' and yet hasn't, in the past, been capable of bringing me to tears. Although I don't appear to be fully in control of my current palette of emotions.

It is understandable given everything that has been happening in the world. And, in addition, there is something about spring which already has my sentimentality on high alert. The stimulus of daylight which begins to stretch out, the scent of warmer air and growth all around has always awoken something – a sensation that might not be immediately obvious, but is certainly there, deep within. It is the feeling of moving on, while also perhaps remembering times past as our journey takes us forward but through the places that seem so familiar because we have visited them before. Spring and autumn always seem to have the greatest power to affect – the two seasons of change and transition.

Conditions, therefore, are ideal for emotional over-spill and it's why I would currently grow weepy listening to anything from *Adagio for Strings* to 'Touch My Bum' by the Cheeky Girls. Indeed, the same musical trigger happened when I was listening to Glen Campbell singing 'Galveston' recently. Again, it's a perfectly pleasant song from the Campbell canon, released in 1969. Yet I found myself thinking about a place in Texas that I have never visited nor likely ever will. More than that, I found myself thinking about a different *time*, imagining what it was like to live then, certain that it would be better than now – *fernweh* with a bit of temporal travel thrown in. But, of course, the selective filter of nostalgia is a powerful distortion. 'Galveston' was written in the midst of and about the Vietnam War. Just a few years earlier you would look at your diary wondering if you could fit in a nuclear holocaust a week on Tuesday. We may be going through a difficult period, but there have been plenty of those in the past and some, not that much further back, which were far more destructive than that offered by our own current adversity.

Perhaps we are also less able to cope now with things not going according to plan. We are softer than our forebears in that we – and I obviously mean those of comfortable means in a developed country in the last fifty years – have never had it so good, as was once said. Or perhaps we are not necessarily a softer generation but just one that has been granted so many opportunities. We are so frequently told we can live the ideal life and have anything and everything we want, that when things fall far short of this ideal we struggle to accept it.

What is happening to us now seems to be very similar to the intensifying of emotions that you experience when travelling on an aeroplane. Even though I haven't been on one of those things in over a year, in a previous life I was a frequent enough air traveller to experience it quite often, usually while watching a film on board.

It is a recognised phenomenon, although the

explanation for it is harder to pin down. Some scientists believe that it is due to the slight reduction in air pressure. Or that it is caused by the feeling of helplessness and the loss of control of the whole flying environment. Others still would suggest that it is due to a fundamental sadness at having to eat a rubberised pasta dish while losing the battle for the armrest with the gentleman in the next seat. Most say that it is a combination of a number of such factors, all of which come together in a perfect storm to make you cry at various points during *Pirates of the Caribbean 2*.

At the moment, we are all living in an aeroplane – sealed in, hurtling through space without much feeling of control. So our moods can swing wildly, becoming borderline euphoric at a nice apple turnover with a cup of tea then moving to incredibly weighed down, a feeling of melancholy or weepiness brought on by a song. Over what exactly, it's difficult to say. It's just an unsettling, existential angst.

Oh, how we bounded into lockdown about this time last year, firmly believing that it was something to embrace. 'It's like…I've been given the gift of time, yeah?' said one of my friends. And I enthusiastically agreed, vowing that I would simply enjoy being free to work on my music, or learn to knit. But of course, like all good things, while a little extra is something to be savoured, a glut can be harmful. And we are certainly a generation that has more time to think – to dwell on our situation and muse over whether or not we are fulfilled. It would always be better to make our way through life occupying our days with whatever work, pastimes and ventures that we see fit and realising only later, if we're lucky, that fulfilment has happened along the way – without too much analysis about our status or the process, or even having to order something from a fulfilment centre.

The problem is that our human brains are incredible (or some of them, at least). A nice problem to have, I grant you, as they can create a vaccine within months or fashion the technology that will take us to Mars. But they also have the power to operate with a depth of thought that is not entirely helpful. And when given too much time, they twiddle their cerebral thumbs and decide to busy themselves with all manner of rumination that we don't really need. 'Am I warm, am I fed, am I safe?' is never enough for us.

So we think…perhaps more subconsciously than at the forefront of our minds, but we think nonetheless. We think about the normal order and structure being broken and how unsettling change can be. We remember how we lived until recently and how we are all now made smaller and less sure of ourselves. We reflect with anxiety for the world as a whole – something which has been lost, an indefinable absence.

But as the song says, sometimes we don't know exactly what it is that frightens us.

And now, I really must stop thinking about it all.

APRIL 2021

Friday 2 April

We are in Cambridge…

In years past this would have felt mundane or matter of fact – now it feels as if we are on a true adventure. Intrepid explorers pushing on towards terra incognita, with the map a blank save the inscription *Here be dragons,* even though I know it's just off junction 13 of the M11.

All four of us have made the trip because I am covering the Boat Race on Sunday. The historic sporting-cum-social event of spring has been moved to the River Great Ouse in nearby Ely from its usual location on the Thames between Putney and Mortlake, owing to the insurmountable problem of boats being forbidden from travelling beneath Hammersmith Bridge, as it has recently been declared unsafe. In addition there is the pandemic, which has also been deemed unsafe.

Olive and Mabel are in attendance because, in a fit of uncharacteristic over-enthusiasm, I suggested to the editor some weeks ago that, for our film of the guide to the course, I could run it with them. Despite the fact that I chuckled as I said it, clearly letting him know that I was not being entirely serious, it struck a chord and he decided to make it a full production as a race between me and my dogs on the land and, out on the water, twice Olympic champion James Cracknell. And so here we are.

The first thing we do on arrival is what should be the relatively simple task of checking into our hotel. Instead, by virtue of Olive's ongoing refusal to walk over hard and shiny floor surfaces, it escalates into something which would qualify as one of the twelve labours of Hercules. You know the sort of thing: Capture the Cretan Bull, Slay the nine-headed Hydra, Get a reluctant Labrador to walk into a pleasant four-star hotel.

Progress is made in long, painfully drawn-out stages. A rug or section of carpet is viewed as some sort of island sanctuary and she will make a shivering, legs-wide scuttle to get there, paws scrabbling frantically, almost producing the sound effect they used to employ in cartoons when somebody started running. Having reached her chosen place of safety, she then refuses to move, lowering her ears flat against the side of her head and gently batting me away with one outstretched paw. Eventually she dashes over to an armchair that sits in the corner of the foyer and lets me know that she would quite like to remain there for the duration of our stay. At this point Hercules would have requested if he might

be allowed to proceed to the next one on the list, suggesting that obtaining the girdle of Hippolyta seems a
more interesting task anyway. But in my own labour it is
the point where a member of staff wanders by, a heavy
frown above the mask, as it appears that I have invited
Olive up there and they pass by muttering, wondering
why their hotel decided to accept dogs.

I do, though, smile as apologetically as I can, already
feeling great sympathy for those who are working here.
They are supposed to be considered among the fortunate ones in that their jobs do at least still exist, but
they now have to operate with such rigour and attention to detail, just to enable the hotel to operate. And,
as part of the uniform, they must wear a visor the likes
of which suggests that between checking in guests they
have a sideline in light welding. All for a few people
staying here while travelling on essential business – such
as that vital work of filming dogs running alongside a
river.

To take Olive out of her deep discomfort zone, we
decide to go for an amble around the streets. Again it
is unquestionably nice to be out, although Cambridge
lies in the same state of altered reality that I have seen
in Belfast and London; usually so busy, it is near empty.
We are also in the midst of the Easter holidays and so
the streets feel even more stripped of life. On the last
occasion I had been here, over a year ago, it was alive
and bustling – with tourists who gazed at spires or

furrowed their brows at maps and with the thousands of students who strolled around, lost only in their elevated thoughts. And, every time my car pulled up at a set of traffic lights, I was quickly surrounded by the cycling masses – as if the peloton of the Tour de France were passing through, just more upright and sedate and with additional chinos and wicker.

The absence of all such normality does at least give us more room today, so we wander around for a while in the spring sunlight, past buildings of ornate, sculpted limestone and with every few steps and in each direction we pass the venerable institutions, carrying names of grandeur – King's College, Jesus, Trinity, Gonville & Caius, and Corpus Christi. These are the rooms or halls which temporarily housed those who have shaped the history of this country and indeed the world. Oliver Cromwell walked these streets four hundred years ago. Darwin began a journey which would explain how we came to exist, Keynes developed ideas which dictated how we all prospered or otherwise. Maclean, Burgess, Philby and Blunt made choices based on a different view of the world, and Oppenheimer passed through heading down a path that came close to rendering all such theories and beliefs irrelevant. You can't help but feel overawed here and very aware of your own sense of time and place – and perhaps insignificance. Not least when I notice that one of the few places open as a dining option today is a McDonald's and I question whether any of those learned figures would ever stoop to contemplating a veggie burger, medium fries and a McFlurry, as I am now. Cromwell, possibly.

Although I can at least share some common ground with one of the great poets who made his mark in this place and beyond. The aforementioned Lord Byron, who would go on to scribble a verse or two while traipsing around Europe, was such an animal lover that he kept a whole menagerie of creatures including a fox, monkeys and a badger, although not necessarily all at the same time.

His greatest affection though – even allowing for Lady Caroline Lamb – was reserved for his dog, a Newfoundland called Boatswain. Sadly Boatswain was a victim of a strictly enforced 'no dogs' policy at Trinity College, yet with the small print in the rules and regulations specifying only dogs, Byron was able to show his frustration the best way he knew how, by arriving at lectures instead accompanied by a bear.

Despite his tendency to the eccentric, one of Byron's later works demonstrates his undiluted love for dogs in general and Boatswain in particular. When his best friend had departed (at the very tender age of five, after contracting rabies), he was buried at Newstead Abbey in Nottinghamshire, in a tomb which is larger than that which would eventually mark the grave of Byron himself. And it carries the 'Epitaph to a Dog', containing the lines:

'...in life the firmest friend,
The first to welcome, foremost to defend,
Whose honest heart is still his Master's own,
Who labours, fights, lives, breathes for him alone'

These are words which may have been amended if Byron had had the chance to meet Olive, who very often does things to please only herself, but I am fully behind him on almost all the other sentiments contained within the work. It does show a fairly sizeable disdain for humans as well, but it is the elevation of the dog that shines through, ending as it does:

'To mark a friend's remains these stones arise;
I never knew but one — and here he lies'

I suppose this would have been rather chastening to anyone who presumed themselves an actual human friend of Byron, but it is the words of one such person, John Hobhouse, which are even better known now by dog lovers than those within 'Epitaph to a Dog'. Introducing Byron's work on the tomb of Boatswain, they describe,

'...one who possessed Beauty without Vanity,
Strength without Insolence,
Courage without Ferosity,
and all the virtues of Man without his Vices.'

Anybody who has owned and loved a dog and felt that loyalty and bond, or the pain of absence after they have gone, will recognise their relationship in the lines of Byron and Hobhouse.

We all feel it. It's just that not every dog is so well connected that they can have a sizeable monument to mark their final resting place in the grounds of a country estate, carrying a work written for them by one of this country's most celebrated poets. You really have to hand it to Boatswain, he clearly made quite an impact in his short life.

As far as I know, nobody wrote a eulogy for the bear.

Saturday 3 April

Off to film our piece today, but only after the early and very necessary sortie round the streets of Cambridge again. In fact, it is thanks to Olive's eagerness to unburden herself this morning that we greatly accelerate the process of crossing the hotel floors, whittling it down to about fifteen or twenty minutes. The next problem is that for dogs who require grass beneath their paws to initiate proceedings, the options outside are limited.

The only greenery nearby seems to be small squares of manicured and forbidding lawns which belong to the colleges and it would be sacrilegious to despoil them. I'm sure that Byron and whichever animal he was dragging round with him that day were far more relaxed about it all, but we continue to search, Olive and Mabel moving with an ever-quickening stride and me occasionally losing the leads of each of them to opposing sides of a lamppost – Hobhouse having failed to point out that they are also *possessing strength without intelligence*. Eventually we find our way down to the common ground by the River Cam and all is well.

But once more seeing this city in the daylight and all the places where people would usually gather brings out a huge feeling of sympathy for students here and at universities or colleges everywhere. Which I accept is not often a widely held sentiment.

Of course, for students there are no fears of losing jobs and the stresses of employment, nor the wider concerns of the more serious, mature world beyond graduation, but this is the one short period of life when your whole raison d'être (apart from the minor intrusion of education) is one of fun and growing socially. Everything is about being out there and meeting people and a certain level of irresponsibility is expected, whether a bear is involved or not. It is a time which doesn't come again and to spend a huge part of it cooped up is a great loss.

We are at least free to go to Ely to shoot a dog-man-Olympic-champion race and eventually we can put it off no longer. I'm nervous because it is quite a production. We will be filmed by cameras behind and in front in cars driving along the towpath, from above with a drone and from a boat on the water where another camera operator will film James, who also has two mini-cameras attached to his scull. And possibly his skull, such is the size of the operation. My usual method of filming Olive and Mabel, employing one slightly battered phone, rather pales by comparison.

When we set off, I do have concerns that Olive might ruin everybody's day with her penchant for simply hanging back and eating grass when I want her to run with me, but as it turns out she is something of a star in the film, with a performance of erratic behaviour which works beautifully. With Mabel trotting alongside me, as is her wont, Olive once more dances to her own tune on a run which plots a more circuitous route via a series of diversions – among them a security guard's sandwich and a quite hearty roll on her back in a dead fish.

In the end it isn't exactly a race as both teams have been seriously hindered. James because the choppy conditions in a keen north wind mean that his scull is rapidly filling up with water. Team man–dog because Olive is rapidly filling up with grass, decomposing pike and the remains of a coronation chicken baguette. But not to worry – that's what editing and the artifice of television is for. I run out of dog biscuits during filming and hope that nobody will notice the final shot of the piece will be Mabel being offered the prize of a chunk of James's cereal bar instead. Which she eventually spits out, to Olive's great delight.*

Sunday 11 April

The final day of commentary on the Masters again, which has returned to its more customary part of the year, yet once more we have been working from the BBC studios. Today, after we finish describing the action, I leave the Georgian spring sunshine and step out into a Salford night with heavy wet flakes of snow falling on the quayside. During the last few days I have had a number of messages asking me if I am enjoying the trip and I reply with a shattering of the illusion of television by telling them that the drive alongside the Manchester Ship Canal was pleasant enough. But it is just the way of the world and if this is how work has to happen for now, then so be it.

And besides, the business of simply going to work – leaving and coming back home again – has at least helped in restoring just a hint of a feeling of normality. Although it has also confirmed something else beyond any reasonable doubt: Olive and Mabel have become clingier than ever. Tonight, as I get back at half past one in the morning, they initially raise rather drowsy and rumpled heads but then, on realising the enormity

---

* I should make mention that Cambridge won both the men's and women's editions of the Boat Race the following day. Olive and Mabel followed it keenly from the sofas at home.

of the situation, leap around and howl and sing while Olive travels back and forth under my seated legs and Mabel performs a stiff-legged staccato jig with her ears somewhere back around her shoulder blades.

In a more subtle, low-key fashion, it is noticeable in the everyday as well. I lose track of the number of times I have gone into a room and, such is the butterfly nature of my brain, comprehensively forgotten what I am there for, so turn round only to trip over one or other of them who has shadowed me and is now asking where I am going, what am I doing and can they be of any assistance in the matter?

Furthermore, there is some time-distortion effect taking place in their heads whereby one minute or one day is considered exactly the same. I go to fetch something from the car and return within moments, yet there they are, standing at the door, surprised at how little I have aged but delighted to see that I hadn't died as they feared, and holding a toy as a gift to ensure I never leave them again.

It must be said that the main culprit in the neediness is Mabel. Olive has always been far more comfortable with a bit of separation. Indeed, often she insists upon it, taking herself away to one of the many sleeping options she has dotted around the house. Yet even she is showing signs of requiring my company more often than before.

When I go upstairs, where she knows she is not

allowed unless invited, she will now wait at the bottom, positioning herself in the widely recognised saddest pose that any dog can muster, lying down with two paws stretched out in front and head between them.

If I have taken myself off to another room downstairs, it is only a matter of time before there appears an insistent and quite powerful snout through the gap in the door, first snuffling to confirm my location then widening it until one or both of them can come in and join me.

Occasionally I feel that I need my own space if I'm trying to work on something, in which case I will take the drastic option of firmly closing the door – and Olive doesn't understand locks or catches. Within a short while comes the clack of claws on the floor, slowly building up speed, followed by a thump as solid Labrador head meets resistance where none was expected. There is clearly a moment or two of quiet contemplation before a whine arrives, which is a mixture of frustration and also feeling a bit sorry for oneself.

So it is important that I do start leaving the house again and getting back to work – to get out of the house myself and to wean them off my awe-inspiring presence. What's more, these current trips into the studio are also a reminder of how much we are social creatures. A few months ago the confident suggestion was made that offices might become a thing of the past – that people could do their jobs from home and that remote working was the way forward. Of course, the vast majority of office-based jobs *can* be done from home but there is no doubt now that the communal aspect of going to an office, seeing and meeting other live human beings is fairly important to our sanity.

Yes, these dogs will just have to get used to my occasional disappearance and I'm sure we will both be better for it. There is forever going to be an advanced level of hysteria on my return either from sunny distant lands or the snows of Salford. But I make sure to say tonight, as I do each and every time I leave, that I will always, always come back to them.

Tuesday 13 April

For once, Olive and Mabel are not the most excited creatures in the house this morning. Caroline comes running down the stairs to let me know that our age group now qualifies for a vaccination appointment and what's more you can book them...BOOK THEM NOW.

So I get straight onto the NHS website and suddenly it's like purchasing tickets for a concert just as they are released and they're going fast. Every time I try to finish the process and click 'Book Appointment', I am told that said appointment is no longer available. So I have to start again and, like the very best seats in the house, good appointments nearby are disappearing. What's more, from recognised medical centres we seem to be moving into any business with the requisite space. At this rate my only option will become a 200-mile round trip to have it out of the back of a van in the car park of a Supasave mini-market – injection to be administered by the local cub scouts. And what's more, I'll gladly take it.

Eventually I get signed up to a hotel somewhere in Liverpool, but I am inordinately happy and keen to share the good news and vital information with everybody. I text my entire catalogue of friends to let both of them know that it is possible for the over-45s to book an appointment as of today. TODAY!

'I had mine two weeks ago,' comes the first reply.

'I've already had both,' says the other.

Wednesday 14 April

There's an offer that keeps returning to my inbox to do special video greetings for people. This is now a reasonably big business – well-known folk sign up with one of the companies and then people can buy a personalised video message from them. This could be a sports star or TV presenter saying Happy Birthday, Get Well Soon, Congratulations on your Graduation or Wedding or Parole.

Investigating further (never rule anything out immediately), I see that there is a sliding scale of cost for each celebrity, which would leave you in no doubt where you stand. They start at as little as £10 – who you get for that I'd rather not say – and move up to £750 and beyond. Needless to say, the offer is for me to do these flanked by Olive and Mabel; on my own I understand that I would create a whole new price plan at the bottom end of the market. But wherever we are ranked, it's not something that appeals.

I do and have done quite a number of messages for individuals who have got in touch, still only a tiny number of all the requests which come in because you haven't got time – just a few of them that seem more meaningful than others. But I certainly don't want to charge for it. It feels not unlike signing an autograph, returning the pen and then holding out your open palm, while coughing expectantly.

People still have to make a living though and with a message lasting no more than thirty seconds, a celebrity might take ten minutes or so out of their busy (or now less busy) celebrated life to record about twenty and so perhaps you can understand why they do it. What's more, there are a huge number of performers listed there – actors, singers, comedians – who will have been unable to do any work at all in recent months with theatres closed and a good deal of television and film production halted. So why shouldn't they earn something for it? Once more it is a case of humans adapting well to the change in circumstance and an overriding need to pay for groceries.

Of course, if you do sign up, there is the danger of a significant dent to morale, as you realise that your true value places you just below a children's entertainer from the late seventies who most people thought had died. And you also run the risk of further ridicule – it seems particularly relevant today as I see that former politician and general mouth-for-hire Nigel Farage (£75 per recording apparently) has made quite an impact with one of his messages, staring into his phone camera and breezily sending happy birthday wishes to one of his very biggest fans, Hugh Janus. Still, as we said – everybody has to make a living.

Thursday 15 April

In the graph of happiness index, the curve certainly appears to be upward. Not only is the weather dry and sunny with spring weaving its mood-improving magic but, for a few days now, further essential businesses have been allowed to open again, in England at least. And two of those resurrected trades which seem to be attracting most of the attention are pubs and hairdressers.

Of course, how essential they are really depends upon the individual. In recent years I have had little call to go into either since I have never been much of a drinker – either social or fully committed – and haircuts have involved shearing myself, like a sheep with increasingly thinning wool, every two or three weeks.

As is often the way, I decide to chronicle the latest development through the medium of Olive and Mabel – or at least I am inspired to do so by Mabel on our walk this morning, plunging into a muddy ditch beside

Cheltenham Literary Festival. It was a rehearsal,
which explains the empty seats. I think.

(Almost) stars of the West End.

The specially created outdoor studio on BBC Breakfast, with Louise Minchin.

Lockdown hobbies. Mabel works on her music.

The familiar look of those forced to play board games at Christmas.

Eau de Damp Dog. Getting artistic on Formby Beach.

A long-awaited release into the mountains. Mabel
with her tongue of concentration.

The Twa Dogs sculpture. Faithfully recreated by only one of ours.

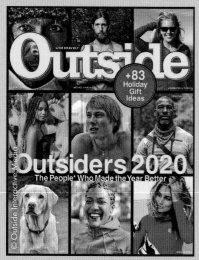

Outsider of the Year in the USA.
Olive left out entirely.

But winning Tongue of the Year.

Filming a race by the River Great Ouse for the BBC Boat Race coverage.

On *The Great Food Guys* with Nick Nairn and Dougie Vipond.
Typically different approaches to food from Olive and Mabel.

With other blond and dark-haired colleagues. Boris Becker
and Tim Henman in Centre Court commentary box.

Mastermind.

And to them perhaps I am.

The Olympics – how the Tokyo studio really appeared. Athletics commentary concentration with Steve Cram and Steve Backley. And two champions in their own strange sport.

Access All Areas at the PGA Championship. Nobody ever misspells Olive.

Always leave the audience wanting more. Or never leave,
because you want more snacks from them.

the track. She emerges very pleased with herself and distinctly two-tone, giving the impression of wearing four thigh-high leather boots. Most dogs at this point in proceedings would either be scolded or dragged to the nearest water to rinse them immediately and cleanse them of their sins. Instead, I warmly congratulate Mabel and reach for my phone as the mud hardens and both dogs stand patiently, their walk interrupted by a process with which they are all too familiar. Later on, junior dog is rather less tolerant as we have relocated back to the house for the second part of filming, which involves a basin of water and a sponge. Olive is allowing herself a wry smile away to the side, very happy to be playing only a supporting role in this one.

Among all the nice comments that follow the video's release are a good number remarking how gentle I am in dabbing away at Mabel and some pointing out that my dog-cleaning method seems to be largely ineffective. I choose not to tell them that this is because I had only one hand free and that once the camera stopped rolling, she was jet-washed with the kind of force used to strip graffiti from walls.

Again, I ponder on the exact reason why I make these videos at all, but the reaction and the feeling it brings from others and from within me is enough to quieten any deeper analysis.

Almost as if knowing that I am in need of an answer, my email provides one later in the evening, with correspondence arriving from a man who tells me that Olive and Mabel are responsible for him and his partner getting together. Last year, he was sent one of the videos and decided to pass it on to a childhood love from whom he had drifted apart and hadn't spoken to in years. Thankfully she didn't reply with 'What is this crap?' or 'The restraining order also includes messaging, Stuart' and things reignited from there. He adds that they are now in the process of buying a house together.

I am glad to have contributed and ask nothing in return except that they call their firstborn Andrew – even if it is a girl. Mabel is now looking out a hat for the wedding and is very glad that she has had her hair done.

Friday 16 April

In this ongoing week of progress, I have become one of the vaccinated millions.

Somewhere deep within, the training process has started. The process whereby my immune system is now being educated to identify something called a spike protein on the virus and furthermore recognise that this is bad. It is effectively me pointing at one of the sofas where Olive is not allowed to sleep overnight, holding up incriminating black fur in the morning and saying 'NO. Nooooooo' over and over again in a stern voice until she realises that this is wrong. Although clinical trials of this preventative method have offered disappointing results for some years now and we are in danger of losing our government funding.

In any case, I now feel invulnerable. Or sixty per cent less vulnerable at least. And it's intriguing to see how matter-of-fact this strange situation is becoming as the vocabulary enters common parlance. We chat to others about the process in the same manner that we would discuss sport, or the weather, or the dreadful roadworks on the M6. Asking which vaccine you had has become a question akin to asking what car you drive or where you go (used to go) on your holidays. If you say Astra Zeneca, people are likely to look slightly underwhelmed as if you own a Vauxhall Insignia. Whereas others will elicit nods of approval.

'Mmm…Moderna. That's a good one. But I heard you can only get it if you're under twenty-five or live in Wales.'

In terms of vaccines I admit to driving the Vauxhall, but I might start saying that I had a Russian one specially imported and that I now feel oddly compelled to go to military bases and take photographs every now and again. Or maybe I'll just be grateful that I'm able to have anything at all.

I have also become aware of the mistake which can be made in discussing where people are in the vaccination process, since it is done by age and the younger you are, the longer you will have to wait for an injection. Misjudge the situation by suggesting, 'You'll have had your second one then,' and watch a face tighten and feel the room temperature fall in the same manner as asking, 'When's it due?' without quietly checking with somebody else first.

On this auspicious day, rather fittingly, it is also the day when we administer Olive and Mabel's latest dose of worm medicine. As I have discussed the irrational fears of our dogs in great detail in previous publications, I won't dwell much longer on it. Suffice to say that Olive has long been an anti-vaxxer in this regard and stages her own sit-in protest in the corner of the room, once more using walls to aid her defence, with Mabel wandering around holding a rubber bone aloft like a placard, even though she seems to rather enjoy the procedure.

So ardent is Olive in her upset and non-compliance that I fully expect her to be on dog chat forums later tonight, spreading misinformation about the worm medicine – that it contains spying technology and that the Kennel Club can watch your every move. I decide it's best not to tell her about the actual chip contained within the rolls of her neck, easily enough put there by a vet many years ago who simply distracted her with a small snack.

Tuesday 20 April

EMAIL
From: Andrew Cotter
To: Expensive Swedish Tent Company
Subject: Complaint

To whom it may concern,

I wish to draw your attention to the one-person tent within your range – which I purchased at no small cost – and express disapproval in the strongest possible terms about your description of said tent as offering 'great levels of comfort'. I, as one person, have just endured a deeply uncomfortable night. Nowhere in your promotional literature did it mention that a one-person tent should not also involve the company of two medium-sized and confused dogs.

Yours sincerely,
Andrew Cotter

I am happy. It happens every now and again. But today I am happy because I am back in the Highlands – back in the mountains for the first time in eight months. With Olive and Mabel in tow, I am meeting our regular human hiking companion, Iain Cameron, for an eagerly anticipated expedition as we aim to walk deep into the hills, camp overnight and then tramp our way over

Beinn a' Bhùird and Ben Avon, two of the more isolated summits on the high plateau of the Cairngorms.

There is, to temper the high spirits, a morsel of concern as my plans often reveal themselves to be very much better in my head than when put into practice. Indeed, somewhere deep inside my mind lies a well-stocked repository of overambitious ideas, all returned with the complaint 'not as advertised'. Camping certainly has the potential to be a prime example of this. Camping with dogs even more so.

In your head you only have idyllic images of how it is going to be, but the first problem is that thoughts and visions weigh nothing and as we set off from the cars, reality grabs the ideal by the collar and slaps it rudely about. This is owing to all the extra gear involved – a lot of it for the dogs and none being carried by those who require it. The walk-in might only be five miles or so and doesn't involve too much ascent, but it still calls for serious effort with thirty kilos to carry. Olive and Mabel cavort around, unburdened by anything physical or mental.

Yet even with one large and one smaller rucksack lashed together and strapped to my back, I have had to forego a couple of items, doing without a sleeping mat and making room instead for a thick children's sleeping bag on which the dogs will be able to lie tonight. It does appear to be made from materials somewhere far beyond polyester on the artificial spectrum, but they'll be quite happy. I can cope with my own discomfort as I know why I'm putting myself through it; I couldn't really handle them being uncomfortable.

When we eventually reach as suitable a camping spot as we can find, we then pass around half an hour trying to clear and level the ground, with the dogs offering little assistance. In fact, many of the loose items which I have moved away promptly return in the mouth of Mabel, who helpfully drops them at my feet and looks at me as if expecting praise for her contribution. Equally, in pitching the tent, their input is enormously counterproductive – both dogs wandering around and either getting in the way or having an ill-timed brawl, and in the process tripping over guy ropes and dislodging the pegs so that the tent slowly deflates like my hopes.

When finally my work is done, I admire the structure as if I have built the great pyramid of Cheops and proudly show the dogs their sleeping quarters. Olive and Mabel appear underwhelmed, suggesting that while this has been a mildly entertaining diversion, they would now very much like to know where their comfortable hotel is, complete with a roaring log fire and a sofa.

In fact, before too long there is at least a fire. Iain has travelled with a pit that stands on a tripod, so we take care to douse the surrounding ground with water and, after such a dry month, no end of perfect wood is quickly gathered – Mabel almost proving herself useful by collecting sticks, but then dropping most of them near to Olive, who chews them into small, useless crumbs of wood and drool.

The other task the dogs perform is to pester me constantly, as it's well past their normal feeding time and they point out that they have worked very hard carrying nothing at all on the long walk in. So I lighten my rucksack by a couple of kilos and serve up dinner to their immeasurable delight, and then fire up the stove to set about feeding myself.

As a humbling admission from a lover of the outdoors, camping is not something I do very often; I have been raised as soft as my dogs and would rather set out into the hills on a day raid from my car or, if I do have to stay overnight, like Olive and Mabel I prefer the home comforts of a cottage or a Bed and Breakfast, the very name of which is enough to sell the idea to the dogs. But there is no doubt that in the right conditions and in the correct frame of mind, a tent and a fire gives you all you need and so much more in terms of an experience.

It's clear we have made the right decision here as we sit, lie or crouch by the fire. Olive, relaxed and warm, slowly closes her eyes and Mabel more alert, cocks her head when it crackles and spits or stands rigid, on guard, when an owl sounds not too far away.

This is where the primeval connection between us as creatures is laid bare. You think of these descendants of wolves and the origins of how dogs and humans came to live together as inseparable companions. It appears that the divergence of wolves and dogs occurred between twenty and forty thousand years ago when the reach of ice in the Northern Hemisphere was at its peak. With the kind of vagueness that palaeontologists sometimes display, we are told (and I can almost imagine the breezy wave of the hand) it occurred 'somewhere in Europe or Asia'. What we are certain of is that the climate was a lot colder, but meat was plentiful for human hunter-gatherers and a few bold wolves decided they had to step up their scavenging game – or even invent a new game called begging – so wandered closer to habitations. Rather than impale them for yet more food to stock up the freezer beside the mammoth steaks and gigots of sabre-toothed tiger, those early humans shared some meat, possibly scratched an ear, and it all began. A bond forged. Dogs have seen us as providers of comfort and snacks ever since.

But there is something perfect and very simple about it: how much we both get out of the relationship and have done for those thousands of years. So here we are, with the fire lifting into a sky still light at the edges where it meets the sharp black lines of the mountains. The moon is bright with only Venus for company but the sky gradually darkens and one by one a few more stars begin to appear. Somewhere up there, if I could identify it, is Mars and a small, industrious rover busying itself on the surface. Far below, we all stare into the flames and it feels right to both man and beast.

The heat, though, only travels a few feet and beyond its reach the temperature is dropping fast. As I clear things away, my fingertips start to numb with the cold and on a clear April night with winds coming from the north, I hope we're going to be warm enough.

Inside my poorly constructed accommodation, it doesn't feel too bad at all, yet the issue with camping is always the chill seeping up through the floor of the tent from the ground below. It remains to be seen how much of a defence Olive and Mabel's electric-blue acrylic sleeping bag is going to be, but I've seen them snoozing in snow holes before and dogs are masters in the art of keeping themselves warm. Or at least, one of ours is. Olive very quickly taps into the knowledge of her ancestors and shapes herself into the most impressive tight ball – she is now just a perfectly round shadow in the corner of the tent. Eyes shut, nose firmly wedged in her rear and tail wrapped around like a perimeter fence, there is no way to tell where she begins and ends. The wagons are circled and nothing can permeate her thick, black fur.

Like many other supposedly inherent dog tricks of the trade, Mabel hasn't quite mastered the technique – a rather shoddy effort leaves a gap here or there in her perimeter fence. In ancient times she would have been laughed out of the pack. What's more, every time the wind picks up outside, the gossamer fabric of the tent comes to life, rippling and snapping, at which point her head lifts and eyes widen as if worried that she has angered the gods in some way and she looks to me for reassurance. So I remove an arm from my own warm cocoon and scoop her in closer, which seems to ease her immediate fears.

But you can still see her small and anxious mind at work. 'Am I fed? Am I warm? Am I safe?' With only one of those boxes currently ticked, it may be a long night, short on sleep.

Wednesday 21 April

A thick layer of frost covers the outside of the tent and even the water bottles in the small tent porch rattle with chunks of ice inside. But the lightening sky promises grand weather and so, at the behest of Olive, we rise about 4.30 a.m. and all go through our downward dog morning stretches using varying degrees of natural talent. Elder dog seems to have slept best of all and as a result is decidedly perky. Mabel has been fretting most of the night but still seems raring to go because she is fuelled by youthful enthusiasm. I summon what energy I have from my accumulated total of ninety minutes' sleep.

Once again I show my true standing in the pack by preparing the dogs' breakfast first and then, once they have gulped it down without pause, cook up my own on the stove while they lap away at the water in the nearby burn, which comes down fresh and cold from the snow-melt up above.

Olive returns to see what additional food might be

on the menu and for once gets it entirely wrong. She busies herself for a good few minutes digging away in pursuit of a single baked bean which fell off my plate some time ago and, so distracted, misses the far more profitable route taken by Mabel, who gets her nose into the pot. Olive eventually looks up, triumphant, having captured the grass-covered bean and stares suspiciously at her young friend, whose pink nose is tinged with a red sauce. But all of us fed, we are ready to go.

Thankfully we are able to leave the tents here, with most of the equipment inside and travel far lighter up the mountain. What's more, with no deer or sheep or creatures of any great size on the ground, Olive and Mabel are unshackled and leap through the heather and in and out of whatever running water courses they find – every time Mabel racing back to us, giddy with excitement as if reporting the discovery of the source of the Nile.

In all of this they are only reflecting our own feeling – an overwhelming joy at being set free and one which many people are now having the chance to experience. This does bring its own issues of course. As we climb, warming up with both sun and heart rate rising, Iain tells me of events on the previous weekend, the day after travel had been allowed to all parts of Scotland. With the release of everybody who had been cooped up for so long, came the inevitable crowds heading to the mountains and a fair few of them making their way – as he did – to Ben Lui and the peaks nearby. It is one of the most accessible mountains in Scotland, only an hour or so from Glasgow and visible from the busy A82. Still a fair walk to get to the climb itself, but drawing people in with its appearance of Alpine grandeur, which is not misleading.

The majority looked well equipped and well prepared for what lay ahead, but as he was packing up his own gear back at the car, having started very early in the morning, he was approached by a man wearing standard trainers and tracksuit trousers and with a question.

'Is this the way to Ben Lewis?'

'Ben Lui? Aye it is... Going up there, are you?' asked Iain with a justifiably sceptical air, as the man's partner wandered into view. She was also apparently expecting to climb the mountain and what's more would do so clutching her handbag.

'You know there's still quite a bit of snow higher up.'

'No bother. Is it far then?'

And off they went. They may well still be up there.

Of course, I understand it – one of the great equalities of Scotland is that the countryside is open to all with no hill or mountain off-limits. You do hope that everyone also respects the environment and appreciates how dangerous it can be, but if people have been denied movement and space for so long, the desire to get out there will be overpowering. Even if it means a broken ankle or stage two hypothermia in the process.

Again, I'm glad I am not experiencing it in any similar communal way. It was asked of me before I left that, denied of human company for so long, why would you want to take yourself deeper into the wild, further away from people? Because, I replied, we've been living in a chattering, closed-in, artificial world for the past year. We now need that feeling that there is nothing around us but silence. Nothing above but a vast sky. We need that sensation of being in an environment which is entirely natural and organic. Entirely...real. And yes, also because I'm fairly antisocial.

So we carry on in search of whatever it is that we need. Gradually gaining more and more height, Olive and Mabel discover to their glee the significant snowfields which remain and hit them with their usual enthusiasm but, until the sun can do its thawing work, the surface is still rock hard after such a cold night and they do little more than skitter across it. And soon we are on one of the enormous plateaux of the Cairngorms – a remnant of a once massive mountain many times higher, worn away by the repeated advance and retreat of ice over millions of years and two small figures, with two even smaller beside them, now creep across it – tiny in scale of space and time. Here you realise how unimportant everything else seems and how fleetingly we are here – humans and dogs and their shared company no more than a flicker in the eye. I make sure to stand for a while. The pixels and the screens and the electronic lights slip away as I take in the space and the quiet. Listen to the silence. Stare at the wide, unbroken horizon.

It all makes for a long, circular route, eighteen miles alone on this second day, but for every step and a few more of their diversions besides, Olive and Mabel are with us – clearly loving their own return to the wild but at the same time never quite able to break free from their domesticity. I pour water into a bowl or feed them small chicken pieces at every stop and they know they've made the right choice.

When we finally get back to the tents, I start to dismantle last night's shelter and pack it all away. Olive and Mabel are once more offering a modern re-enactment of their ancestors and they scratch at the ground as wolves. But after the day's efforts they are doing it only out of a sense of duty to that deep-rooted DNA and manage no more than a cursory wave with a paw at the turf and one half-hearted circle, before falling asleep almost as they keel over.

While they doze on the now-warm grass, I accept that this is one of the last epic mountain walks I will do with Olive – we are both in human and dog equivalents of middle-age and she will now accelerate away from me into advanced years. But the reasons why I do it couldn't be more clear: to give them the best lives we can and for this feeling which I have as I watch them sleep. When both dogs eventually depart, I will have a vast selection of memories to call upon. Our time may be fleeting, but it can also be rich with experience.

After a joyous day and a half, suddenly the world

seems bigger – it seems better. For once the reality has more than lived up to the ideal.

Friday 30 April

A four-day long weekend social media boycott has begun.

Even if it is unlikely to change a thing, it does highlight how strongly people feel about the state of affairs in this clamorous quarter of our online world.

The wonderful appeal of Twitter (for we can be honest and identify it as the most wayward of the social media family) is that anybody can connect with anybody else. As well as enabling people to remain in touch with each other, it also offers a window into the lives of well-known figures. Twenty years ago, if you wanted a window through which you could view a certain celebrity, then it would have to be their actual window via a telescopic lens or after clambering up a drainpipe – which was frowned upon by both the celebrities in question and the law. Now, you can not only see what they are up to (or at least the bits they want you to see), but you can contact them as well without fear of detention. They might even respond. But that ease of contact is also the downside. It is now such a remarkably simple process to have a notion and immediately fire off a thought or two – perhaps a shrewd observation, a gentle critique on a performance, or a line or two of racism, misogyny and holocaust denial.

I'm well aware that not everything in the human world can be directly translated into the animal kingdom, but the equivalents are there. The herd that gathers, or the flock which comes together after mass migrations. And, when an enormous group of dogs find themselves meeting on a walk, along with the friendly greetings and general tail-wagging, there will always be one dog looking suspiciously at the rest – most often a terrier, on the fringes, shouting abuse. Although he would say that he is just sharing his thoughts and opinions. You can do your best to reason with him and understand what it is that has made him that way, or you can just ignore him and let everybody else have a nice time.

Because, despite all the ills within it, there are thousands, if not millions, for whom social media is a marvellous thing. They use it in the purest form of its original intention – as a source of entertainment, or as company and a community. Since the creation of social media – and in particular during the last year – it has been a vital counter to loneliness for a lot of people. It is where you trade news, jokes, opinions, occasional films of dogs playing poker and a few more opinions. But above all, it offers a connection, something that is just a fundamental requirement of being a human.

As it happens, I will stay off social media today and for the rest of the weekend – not because I am adhering to a boycott, but because I don't really have anything to say or an urgent desire to see what anybody else is saying at the moment. And besides, there is the fundamental requirement of dogs which I have to satisfy by taking Olive and Mabel out again. Although I might put them in the car and take them somewhere different tonight, because there's a collie in a garden down the road who always says some deeply offensive things as we walk by.

MAY 2021

Tuesday 4 May

Today I finally posted the video of our climb in the Cairngorms and I admit – in the pages of this diary at least – to being quite pleased with it. There's a change of tone, while hopefully keeping the humour as I chat away to both Olive and Mabel during the expedition. But it has taken the dogs from claustrophobic sketches in and around our house to the wide-open spaces and, with a bit of help from the footage gathered by Iain's drone camera, it certainly has, in parts, a cinematic quality. It also offers something of an explanation for the way I feel about these dogs and about being out in the mountains with them.

The response is quite something. Views rapidly climbing towards a million on Twitter alone and comments in the hundreds, expressing their approval and with every one of them a dopamine spike hits my brain. This is where you have caught the wave.

But with all of it comes unwelcome and possibly unnecessary self-examination. If we are released from the grip of the pandemic and let loose in the world again, why do I keep on making the videos? After all, in this instance I went climbing to escape the modern world and yet at the same time I took it with me.

I reassure myself that when I am up there, I really am soaking it all in with my own senses and enjoying it for those moments in themselves. But I am also taking photos and filming the dogs – and these captured images are only partly for me to enjoy later on. If I am honest, mostly they are so that I can post them on social media or, in this case, put together this video. There's no doubt I enjoy sharing the trip with others, but what *is* that enjoyment? Do I need the approval? Is this just a superannuated version of every selfie taken by every person hoping that it will generate a thumbs-up and perhaps a word of praise?

But, as with most things we experience just now, I am surely analysing it too much. You might as well ask why people make television programmes or films or write and perform comedy or songs. They do it for themselves of course and their own enjoyment of creating something, but also for the reaction those creations bring. And if that reaction is positive and it strikes a chord with others or cheers them up or moves them somehow, then surely it is worth doing.

A few days ago a man in New Zealand had been in touch on Twitter to say that his daughter checks YouTube every single day to see if there might be a new Olive and Mabel video. So who am I to say no to somebody's child on the other side of this increasingly strange world?

Although I do suggest that perhaps it would be wise for her to only check every three or four days at the very most.

Thursday 6 May

More reports today that incidences of dog theft are on the increase. Thankfully our two are not that desirable to anybody but us, Labradors being ten a penny. Unless, as celebrity dogs, they are going to be kidnapped like the Lindbergh baby, or John Paul Getty II. Or perhaps taken in by a Kathy Bates-style superfan. But French bulldogs everywhere are now being kept on a very short lead. It is heart-wrenching to see the number of people who have had their dogs stolen and I can't imagine what a state I would be in if either of our two were lifted. Thefts in the UK have risen by 250 per cent during the pandemic.

As a result, there is all manner of advice being offered by the police and the Blue Cross on what you should and shouldn't do to reduce the risk of your beloved pet disappearing, including the following:

1. *Have your dog microchipped.*

Absolutely essential. It was one of the first things we did, back when Olive and Mabel still saw the vet as a harmless acquaintance who simply lived in a house full of many animals.

2. *Do not have your dogs' names on their collars.*

Also very sensible advice. This is to prevent would-be thieves from simply summoning your dog – calling them over, presumably with the dog thinking, 'Hmmm, apparently this guy *knows* me. Can't think where I've met him and embarrassing that I can't remember his name, but let's go and bluff our way through it.' However, I would only wish you good luck with that theft technique on our dogs. Even if we did have their names written helpfully on a tag, any potential dognapper might become as frustrated as we do when we try to summon them, giving up after five or ten minutes as they resolutely continue to do whatever they want.

Again, this is probably because they scarcely recognise their own names as, throughout their daily lives, the mentions of 'Olive' and 'Mabel' have to battle for airtime with any number of affectionate monikers such as 'Chops', 'Diggle', 'Plum', 'Mouse', 'Chump' and 'Noodle'. Of course, any thief wishing to bypass this problem with a Labrador only has to be wise enough to have some sort of foodstuff with them. Olive would gladly climb into the back of the van herself before asking to be taken wherever more could be found.

3. *Look out for any strangers asking too many questions on a walk.*

This is hard to identify, since almost everybody we meet asks questions, although 'Is this Olive and Mabel?' and 'Can my Bertie have a photograph with these superstars?' probably aren't quite the questions that the police and Blue Cross are getting at.

4. *Do not post too many pictures or videos of your dogs on social media.*

Wise words indeed, as pictures and videos online are effectively adverts for dog thieves. But with regard to Olive and Mabel, I think that ship has probably sailed.

Friday 7 May

Extraordinary snow for this time of the year has arrived in the Highlands. The mountains where we were just a couple of weeks ago, drenched in sun with only the spring covering remaining, are now clothed in a deep white.

Meanwhile, the positive reaction to the video has continued unabated. A lot of people take it to be an end to the Olive and Mabel series. I hadn't necessarily meant it that way, but there had certainly been a thought that it might be a nice way to bow out. All three of us released into the wild. The happy ending and going out on top.

You don't want to drag things on beyond their natural shelf life and one of the worst things would be to hear either, 'This thing is old/not funny anymore/why is he still doing this?' I do have a couple more ideas, but perhaps it is best to let it go – to move on. You have to at some point.

In the afternoon I head into town for an optician's appointment. And also really just to make a trip into a town. Seeing people milling about, shopping and browsing, getting coffees or lunch is so encouraging.

Less encouraging is the news from the optician, who is already viewing me suspiciously after he asks me what I do for a living and I reply, 'A mixture of sport and dog videos.' I then tell him that I have read on the internet all about screen time being damaging for eyesight and suggest to him that that might be the cause of a recent worsening. To which he sighs, as if he might have heard this amateur offering before.

'No, it's just that you're getting older, I'm afraid.'

'But, the screens...my phone...and the blue light,' I squeak, rather pathetically.

'No... You. Are. Getting. Older,' he says, just a little more firmly this time.

Monday 10 May

We are currently having some landscaping work done in the garden. Free of charge and provided by a mole. Possibly more than one mole, but apparently they are loners, so it is more likely just one, who is nevertheless quite industrious.

Every morning there are a few new heaps of earth in a distinct pattern, from which it's obvious to see his or her commute to work and back, like a subterranean Central Line. Occasionally there is a diversion as if a wrong turn might have been taken, but largely the mounds follow the same path. A friend with greater gardening knowledge has suggested that drastic action is necessary and that I should be looking at fumigation, or other forms of capital punishment, whatever they may be.

Again, this is where I let myself down as a supposed person of the countryside. I think I'm meant to be seeing various flora and fauna as pests – invasive and troublesome to our human development, getting in the way and removable by all necessary force. But I can't. The mole, and any other animal you care to mention, is just doing what we all are – working its way through life as best it can. Of course, I expect now to receive a delegation of local invertebrates asking me to reconsider my position on the matter – aghast that I should care so much about the moles, one of which can apparently eat its own bodyweight in worms every day.

Seeing the landslide and now the mole damage, Olive has decided that it must therefore be a free-for-all in these parts and has started digging in the lawn, working at three very particular holes close to each other and returning to them almost every time she is out there. What it is that she is trying to get at I have no idea – possibly a cowering worm who has seen some dreadful sights. So today I lie in wait, peering from behind a bush until she appears, looks around a couple of times to make sure the coast is clear and then plods over to her site. There is nothing frantic in her method of excavation, rather she proceeds very carefully as if on an archaeological dig. She is methodical, focused and therefore suitably startled when I leap out to give her an enormous bollocking. Chastened, she then retreats to a corner of the garden and lies down, pointedly facing away from me, sighing heavily and no doubt contemplating my enormous hypocrisy – she could easily point out that she is also just doing what she has to do to get through life.

I am, however, increasingly protective of the grass and I realise that this is it... It's happening – I am becoming a gardener. Perhaps it is an age thing as one drifts inexorably towards this sort of behaviour: cutting back the wisteria and tending to herbaceous borders, interspersed with occasional bridge evenings and aqua aerobics. But more likely it is simply that the gardening opportunity has never arisen before in my various stages of life. Or if it did, I chose to ignore it.

Childhood: Not my concern. Gardens just happen

*and I'll reap the benefits. Often by swinging a golf club
and removing enormous chunks of turf.*

*University: What? Why would I have a garden?
Gardens are for ancient people.*

*Twelve years in London: I really would like a gar-
den. But impossible as I'm not a Russian billionaire or
Bernie Ecclestone.*

*Next ten years: Garden of approximately four-
teen square feet. Mowed the grass. Once pulled out a
dandelion.*

Now, though, we do have a garden worthy of the
name. And, while I am never going to be an expert,
I am certainly taking more of an interest. For example, in surfing the radio stations in my car the other
day I even chanced upon *Gardeners' Question Time*
and didn't immediately swerve into a hedge (common
privet, I believe) as I hammered at the controls to find
an alternative. What's more, I then found myself nodding sagely, or generally making interested noises such
as 'Hmmm...' or 'Is that so?' as they discussed the best
techniques for dead-heading.

I am gathering only a superficial knowledge, which
is how I tend to operate in most spheres. I have an
app that helps me to identify plants and flowers without ever imparting any further wisdom and, like most
online assistance, it renders the inconvenient effort of
memorising a fact unnecessary. My phone now does
most of my thinking for me. What I can do is point and

say 'Lovely Forsythia there...' without ever understanding anything more about it.*

There is also an obvious element of escape in a garden. It is having our own space, set apart from the outside world – that feeling of our own fiefdom, which we can control and shape as we want. Although perhaps I'm reading too much into it and it's just a nice place to sit. But while we might sometimes feel that everything outside is getting away from us, here we can act as a benign ruler, dictating the order of things. That is, up to a point, determined by our ability to use tools and put in the effort – I have already issued a decree that certain areas will be left as a 'managed wilderness' because I can't be bothered to get the strimmer out of the shed.

So I wander round on my royal tours, inspecting the flowers and making small talk with birds and insects, who laugh politely at my jokes. Olive and Mabel are in attendance as part of my entourage and I occasionally stop to pick up and put in a bag the gifts that my ladies-in-waiting have left for me – something no monarch should really have to do. Nor should royalty have to cut

---

* After writing this my interest was piqued and so I did some further reading on Forsythia. And I'm glad I did, as I discovered the Forsyth after whom it is named is William Forsyth, an eighteenth-century botanist from Aberdeenshire who became head gardener for the Royal Family and was a founder of the Royal Horticultural Society. Perhaps even more interesting is that his great-great-great-great grandson was the entertainer Bruce Forsyth about whom I knew a good deal more. Not least that his ashes are now beneath the stage at the London Palladium – where Olive, Mabel and I have yet to perform.

the grass, but I willingly do that and perhaps pull out a weed or two – sometimes unwittingly a rare orchid as well, because my app got it wrong.

I realise now, in trying to manage my own perfect kingdom which none may enter, what has happened: I have become Australia, which I'm not sure is a healthy approach. The next step is letting in the postman only after he quarantines for ten days in the garage.

Yet, maybe there is something in the old saying that an Englishman's home is his castle, adapted here for a Scot. It is not the most sociable way to exist, but it does offer a feeling of security and control. So it is into this garden that I now retreat. I pull up the drawbridge and the world outside can't touch or trouble us. Here, I am the Creator and Master of all that I survey.

Except for the moles. I do answer to them.

Wednesday 12 May

The day begins as many do now – with an early morning alarm call from Olive.

At 5.28 a.m. a wet black nose, lying at the end of a long and very insistent black snout, nudges my face, carrying a sock which she has carefully selected from the nearby laundry basket. Most often sleep is abruptly ended by a forceful barking session from downstairs, but last night I obviously forgot to properly close the door to the room where they sleep. Thus, when the first light hits the windows and Olive decides that she and she alone has slept enough, she is able to escape and come and report the marvellous news about the open door.

Though I love my senior dog dearly, I express my affection on this occasion by telling her to bugger off while patting her gently on the top of her shiny dome as if trying to press a snooze button. A couple of minutes later the head of Mabel appears at the bedroom door as well – more tentative at first, as if suspecting that she's not really supposed to be doing this, but then she realises that there is some safety in numbers so trots in, ears back and wagging her whole body – singing one of her nonsensical songs to start the day.

As both of them circle around, doing laps of the room and chatting to nobody in particular about their exciting plans for the day ahead, I give up and lumber downstairs in the wooden-limbed, eyes-squinting fog of the day's beginnings. They follow at first, tripping me up as they clip my heels, Mabel carrying the orange bone by just one end, dangling out of her mouth like a cheroot, and then they push past in their joy at being let out into the garden – scattering pigeons and one or two crows, alarmed at this unexpected intrusion upon their early seed browsing.

Later on in the day I try to reason with the dogs, asking that they don't do it again since I need my sleep and that it's really quite important to only request a human appearance from 7 a.m. onwards.

But my rationale is wasted. To them my conversation

is generally white noise, heard like the indistinguishable sounds of Charlie Brown's teacher, with 'walk', 'biscuit', 'breakfast' or 'suppertime' the only words that stand out from the trombone riffs. Any of these words, plus a questioning intonation will cause a head to tilt to about forty-five degrees in recognition and expectation. One day I might use the sentence, 'Would you like a biscuit on a walk after breakfast and before suppertime?' to see if I can make their heads spin round entirely like the girl in *The Exorcist*.

Having failed to get my message through, the rest of the day is one of limited energy and minimal achievement. I do notice that today marks a year since the release of the video where I held a Zoom meeting with Olive and Mabel. I know this because my phone tells me so, announcing in grand fashion that 'You have a new memory' and playing out the video and a montage of some unrelated photos without asking my permission. But I have given into the technology and accept that it chooses now what I remember, as well as what I see and hear and think. It's effectively the bloke I used to give a lift to at university who would remove my cassettes and put on his mix tapes saying 'You'll love this', until I eventually had to ask him to get out, without noticeably lifting my foot off the accelerator.

My main objective for the afternoon becomes a siesta. Just twenty minutes will make all the difference I'm sure – thank you Spain for this glorious invention.

Unfortunately, as with an infant, the trick is to synchronise your napping with the more disruptive members of the household and here, as the eyes close and the slow drift into wonderful doze begins, my subconscious mind becomes aware of a presence just a few inches from my face. It is Mabel, an hour before her allocated feeding time, asking me if I have perhaps forgotten.

In the evening, still trying to play catch-up, I decide to take my revenge on Olive and Mabel by waiting until they are enjoying their fourteenth snooze of the day and prodding them awake. 'See? Not much fun is it?' but they only think I've said biscuit at the end of my otherwise white-noise question and leap up, skipping happily to the cupboard where they know they are kept.

And so to bed.

At 9:30.

Friday 14 May

In Aberdeenshire today for the filming of a television programme, *The Great Food Guys*, hosted by chef Nick Nairn and Dougie Vipond who, along with his more recent life as a TV presenter, has had a long career as the drummer with Deacon Blue. There is no surprise that Olive and Mabel are invited – in fact, I'm in little doubt that I am only here as their assistant – but even though they are the main attraction, their chaperone and bed carrier is still greatly hoping that the dogs behave themselves and don't ruin their good name.

Yesterday, partly to take advantage of the trip and also in an attempt to tire them out into a state of meek compliance, I led a small, canine-heavy expedition to climb nearby Mount Keen, the most easterly of the Munros. So I have now, at least, completed the four compass points even if there are still many gaps within.* It is, admittedly, not the most thrilling of all Scotland's peaks, but any time I can climb a hill with Olive and Mabel it is well worth it. Even more so when there are still large snow patches to be found about five hundred feet below the summit, softened by the warm sun when we reached them in the late afternoon, but still cooling on their paws and inspiring a good few minutes of snowball catching, combined with general idiocy.

Yet today it becomes clear that my mission to calm them has failed as the dogs are constant distractions during filming. Olive goes off to stick her nose in some food containers which were on the floor in the corner. Mabel wanders off with less obvious purpose, but doing something which matters greatly to her.

It can't be coincidence that this is when Nick starts to tell me of how he considered instilling discipline in his own two Labradors by enlisting a particularly rigorous

---

* If you are, in any way, wondering about the other extremities of the Munros, they are: Ben Hope (north), Ben Lomond (south) and Sgùrr na Banachdaich, on Skye (west).

dog trainer – a man who had once been in the SAS and who has abseiled out of helicopters with a couple of dogs attached, albeit looking as if they hadn't fully agreed to the procedure. In dog-schooling terms it sounds like he may be one of those teachers who takes no prisoners, even if his previous occupation suggests that he would be more than capable. And apparently one of his golden rules of dog ownership, instruction and potential mastery is that dogs should never be allowed on human furniture. At this point, I think of Olive reducing us to pleading with her to come up and join us on the sofa and realise once more that we have fallen some way short as disciplinarians. The greatest disappointment of which is that there will never be an Olive and Mabel video where we all jump out of a helicopter.

Our wayward dogs go on to spend the recording in either one of their two recognised settings: 'asleep', or 'awake and hoping for sustenance'. Sometimes they are seen in the background with eyes only as slits as they doze in their beds, but more often those eyes are bright and stare intensely – domed heads just visible below the edge of the table on which the scallops and black pudding are being prepared. Eventually their hope, patience and light hypnotism pays off, whereby they are gifted a few crumbs of black pudding and you can almost see their pupils dilate as they take in the atoms of a new foodstuff and register it forever more in their internal log of future desires.

We end the day doing the kind of strange and point-less thing that dog people often do – Nick tries to FaceTime his Labradors or, at least, his wife on their behalf. We are told that the dogs are asleep and so we can't chat to them, and we grudgingly accept this news as if it is the only thing preventing us from having a long and stimulating conversation.

Late in the evening, back at the hotel, we lie on the bed with Olive and Mabel snoring on a blanket along-side us. If the SAS dog trainer ever catches me, I am heading for a stern interrogation.

Sunday 16 May

Today I pause while cutting the grass to have a conver-sation with Simon, our still relatively new neighbour. He is the keeper of a very handsome black Labrador called Dexter, who gallops across to our fence, practi-cally stumbling in his excitement, and greets me in the eager-to-please way of Labradors – shouting, but only to let everybody in the neighbourhood know the good news. What the good news is, he's not entirely sure. He only knows that it's most certainly good news.

Yet very quickly he moves on to asking, 'And who, pray tell, are these lovely young things?' as Olive and Mabel trot into view. Since the former owner of our house didn't have a dog, Dexter's social life has now taken a distinct turn for the better. He draws himself up to his full height requesting that I please extend his compliments to the ladies. I think he may even have combed his hair and is now wuffing away, exaggerating the importance of his job.

Mabel doesn't care for such things and produces quite a deep bark of resistance, stating quite firmly that no means no. Olive simply ignores him and carries on eating some of the bluebells which have appeared in the last few days.

As Dexter then takes it upon himself to bring his A game and approach Olive more directly, Simon and I deal with it all in very British terms – by ignoring the invasive nose and determinedly chatting about any other subject which comes to mind. He indicates that we might have a couple of mallards nesting in our garden. I, raised on Beatrix Potter and Walt Disney, make any number of appreciative and cooing noises as I am very fond of ducks and say that I look forward to seeing the little ducklings waddling along behind their mother. He then goes on to point out that ducks are both very dim and incredibly violent in their sex lives – a fact which both Beatrix and Walt neglected to mention. So I return to the mowing rather crestfallen, but at least glad we have already reached the point where we can discuss such matters with our neighbours. Dexter looks equally forlorn as he watches Olive depart, his own sex life non-violent and indeed non-existent.

Later, shortly after my gardening session has finished, I am bending down to put something into the shiny new dishwasher when my back goes. By which I mean it's still very much there, but also now enormously uncomfortable. I blame a particularly heavy mower, but also my lack of a functioning hamstring, which failed on me about a month ago as I did an entirely unnecessary sprint session.

I therefore spend a good part of the evening rolling around on a massage ball – a process which is hindered by both Olive and Mabel either attacking me, since I am down on the floor and they believe I want to play, or just circling me, occasionally hitting me and each other in the face with happy tails.

So I give up and retire to bed, where I struggle to find any sort of comfortable position. I am also rendered uncomfortable mentally, as I choose to read for a while about the dark and disturbing mating rituals of ducks.

Monday 17 May

We have reached a new stage in the release from it all. Another step forward has been made as rules and regulations are relaxed in England and perhaps the most significant change is that people are allowed to hug one another.

I expect to move seamlessly through this transition and resume my pre-pandemic level of zero hugging, but for many people it means a great deal. Today I watched as two women ran towards each other from approximately fifty yards apart, their squeals of delight so high-pitched and their gallop reaching such a velocity, that I thought they were going to fuse into one as they collided. They then held each other for a minute or so, rocking from side to side and laughing. I'm not sure they even knew each other.

But perhaps those full-on embracers are right to throw themselves back into it with such eagerness; after all, they have science firmly on their side. It's something to do with the 'cuddle hormone', which is not a term often used by respected endocrinologists who prefer to call it oxytocin. (I do feel that scientist and lay-person could have met halfway and called it cuddleisium but for some reason I was not consulted.) Whatever the name, the chemical reaction is the same and it gives an explanation to what we have always known – that physical contact can have enormously beneficial effects.

I notice in my investigation on oxytocin that it is also the hormone released during sex and that supposed sex addicts, possibly with a little assistance from their divorce lawyers, have blamed an addiction to oxytocin for their wandering ways. But even as we come together in a more censor-friendly fashion, oxytocin levels rise and we feel calmer and safer. And it doesn't have to involve physical contact, platonic or otherwise. The chemical is also produced in an act as basic as seeing somebody's smiling face or just making eye contact – two more reasons that our reservoirs of oxytocin have been running dry of late. Put simply, it is the hormone of connection and we badly need more of it.

Even with that knowledge – and permission now

granted – I am not yet embracing everyone I meet, as if working the room in the Hacienda in 1991. Not that hugging would be possible at the moment anyway, as I wince with every step. On a constant feed of ibuprofen, I move around gingerly and can't even bend down. I find I have suddenly been transported to somewhere in my late eighties. Nothing makes you feel more elderly than a bad back and a resulting inability to put on socks.

Thus incapacitated, lying on the sofa tonight and feeling rather sorry for myself, Olive comes in to ask me if I am perhaps depressed at leaving our old house – although this could just be a figment of my ibuprofen-altered mind. But as she hops up beside me and tucks herself tightly in a far corner, keeping her distance and enjoying her own space, I remember the most important part of my studies on oxytocin. By all accounts it is produced when hugging a pet as well, so even though I may possess a chill, northern reserve when it comes to human contact, I can unashamedly wrap myself around her. Olive, by contrast, appears to feel plenty of shame and a good deal of discomfort as I move in, but I simply don't care. This is, after all, a fundamental part of the duties of dogs. I point out that it is right there on page one of her contract and she grudgingly allows permission for me to replenish my low puddle of oxytocin.

Besides, while she might not like to admit it, the enormous sigh of contentment a few moments later betrays her. We are, in fact, both stocking up.

Saturday 22 May

We are trudging through the wettest, coldest May I can remember. The rain washes over us in waves and the landscape is slowly dissolving, the edges of the world softened and blurred into a living watercolour. As a dog owner this brings practical difficulties – having to dry them every time they return from one of their many expeditions is growing ever more tedious and we maintain a complement of four or five towels in permanent rotation for the purpose. As it happens, Mabel is almost impossible to dry. However much effort we put in, it only seems to move the water around her surface, as if mopping the outer shell of a recently emerged submarine, until she tries to deal with matters herself by employment of her dramatic corkscrew-shaking manoeuvre which covers us and the walls, initiating a lengthy inquiry into why she couldn't have done that outside. You might think a hairdryer would be a decent alternative, but you would not be taking into account the fact that both dogs consider the implement to be the work of the devil.

In the end we give up all drying techniques and she trots off to her bed, quite happy to exist in this near-permanent state of dampness, barnacles attached to her underside.

I read in the news today that China has now landed its own rover on Mars – 'Zhurong', named after the Chinese god of fire. These are surely the early days of interplanetary empire-building. Perhaps 'Perseverance' and 'Zhurong' will bump into each other as they try and steer their way past the crumpled remains of 'Fingers Crossed 2' lying in its impact crater, or both get stuck behind 'Curiosity' as it stares, intrigued, at a pebble – thus creating the first Martian traffic jam.

I briefly entertain the idea that it would be quite nice to be on the Red Planet at the moment since it is a place not renowned for its rainfall. True, average Martian temperatures of approximately −80 degrees Fahrenheit would demand an extra layer and decent gloves, but still, it would be better than this. The increasing daylight should be helping us at the moment in our corner of Planet Earth but, as far as I can make out, it is just allowing us to see the rain for longer.

Like a child on a summer holiday, reduced to colouring in or board games when the grim weather sweeps in, I decide to spend some of my quality time indoors by filling in an online application for a United States visa, as my last one – which lies in the recently untroubled pages of my passport – is about to expire. It's rather important that I renew it, as I am supposed to travel to Wisconsin for the Ryder Cup in September but, as the afternoon wears on, I gradually come to accept that I may not have finished the form by then. I diligently tick box after box, declaring that I have never to my knowledge taken part in genocide and also that I am not planning sedition after my connecting flight to Detroit. Asked which state I will be in for the duration of my stay, I am tempted to reply 'confused and angry' but remember that immigration officials are not known for their light-hearted ways. Approximately two hours alone are spent on the process of trying to upload a photo which matches the precise number of pixels required, but finally I am finished and am told that I can now book my appointment at the Embassy, noticing with some concern that the first one available is in March 2022.

It is currently only slightly more difficult to get to Mars.

Tuesday 25 May

After my back went, it has at least partly returned, although it doesn't seem to have brought with it the hamstring or hip, which are still absent without leave. I have now been without the freedom of running for over a month. Being able to cycle is one thing, but that is either withdrawn and fictional – in the garage – or out on the roads, inducing car drivers to ever greater levels of rage. Running is simple and what's more can be done with small furry companions who have no recognised hamstring issues. So a trip to the physiotherapist today has become very necessary.

He asks me how I did it and I tell him about the particularly dynamic movement to put a plate in the dishwasher, but since he is a physio and requires full disclosure, I casually mention the 400-metre reps. He is a former athlete of some repute so I know he'll understand. The grimace and noise he makes through his teeth suggests otherwise.

'Not sure that's the most sensible thing to be doing. You're not getting any younger,' he says, having obviously gone to the same school of blunt truths as the optician and I wonder if they are perhaps in league together – firing off messages and discussing plots as part of a WhatsApp group entitled 'How to greatly lower Andrew's morale'. I'll only know it's a true conspiracy if shop assistants start drawing attention to my grey hairs while I browse in the bakery section of Morrisons.

In fact, two of our pack have medical visits today since Mabel, as well as her tendency to gather barnacles and moss, appears to have developed a slight eye infection. In response to this, any sensible dog owner would just dab away at it with a dampened tissue for a few days until it clears up, but we seem determined to single-handedly pay for the vet's new car, so we have made an appointment and take her in.

As expected, we are told that it is absolutely nothing to worry about and I resist the temptation to counter that it is, because she has a heavy filming schedule lined up and can't possibly appear looking like that. But I don't – instead I simply hand over more money for a small bottle of saline solution. I'm almost sure I can hear them laughing and see high-fives being exchanged as we drive away.

One other event of note today is that Bill Shakespeare – the first man to receive a Covid vaccination, back in December – has died of an unrelated illness. A newsreader in Argentina relays the news, saying that possibly the greatest writer in the English language is no more. In their defence this is at least factually accurate, it's just that they're not the first to that particular story.

Sunday 30 May

One of our friends is able to visit this weekend. Much of her past year was spent in a small flat in London, and 'Lockdown One', as the original part of the trilogy is now known, was not easy.

While there might not have been an official competition to ratify her status, I can say with some conviction that there is nobody in the world who is more fond of dogs than she is and whenever she has been able to arrive in the past, it has always been accompanied by a present each for Olive and Mabel – possibly two. In fact, many of the toys that have featured in Olive and Mabel videos – the stuffed rabbit, cloth bones with their names on, et cetera – have been her doing.

Today she arrives once more as the bearer of gifts, unveiling a small startled-looking owl for Mabel, who immediately carries it around with both great care and great pride, walking up to each of us in turn to let us know that she now has an owl. Olive is presented with a sort of squeaky felt duck which doesn't possess a startled look, but really should do as she takes it into a corner and eviscerates it within five minutes, despite regular squeaking protests from the duck which grow more tortured and then fainter as Olive removes first stuffing and then the squeak itself. Since it was a toy version of a male mallard and I now know what they get up to in their private lives, my sympathy is limited. Olive next sets her sights on the owl, but it is in the protective care of Mabel, and while she may be soft, insecure and somewhat scatter-brained in many things, on the matter of her possessions she is the boss and is quite confident in telling Olive that the startled owl belongs to her and that she can take her toy-killing instincts elsewhere.

At the end of what has, in their minds, been a quite wondrous day – joint first with ninety-eight per cent of all the days they have lived – Olive and Mabel are dozing, each taking up their own sofa and both reclining in equally absurd positions of contentment upside down.

Naturally, I film it and put it out there as a vignette of their contented lives, reasoning that videos don't always have to be clever and creative – sometimes people like to see nothing more than dogs in ridiculous poses. In reply, I am told by a few correspondents that the video has to be unblocked to view it as Twitter has taken action, replacing it with a message announcing that this is 'sensitive content'. Finally, I think; with racism, bigotry and all manner of hatred the scourge of social media, I am glad that they are cracking down on dog indecency across the platform.

JUNE 2021

Thursday 3 June

Travel down to Wimbledon for a morning of filming with Tim Henman. In his widely acclaimed status as Tim Henman, he can seldom move more than twenty yards or so at this place without being stopped for a few minutes of his time. In these situations I tend to hang around, not wishing to intrude on the Tim Henman-centric conversation, but today there is something different as each one of those we encounter diverts for a moment to make special mention of Olive and Mabel. Employees or members of the club, players, coaches, physios – all referring to the dog stuff and quite often along the lines of 'What's that all about then?' to which I have no satisfactory answer. I've already experienced a small amount of this in recent months, but suspect that it is going to happen ever more as I get back out into a busier world.

Later on we happen to bump into Andy Murray, on his way to practise on an outside court, and as he and Tim chat away, I am about to join in with proceedings, feeling a need to ask him how it's all going – how's the hip? Ready for the grass courts? And the new baby? Busy during lockdown then, hahahahaha. No, but seriously, great to see you, champ...when instead he gets the first words in.

'How are Olive and Mabel doing?'

So this is it now. No matter who we meet, I am the human sidekick, existing only as an adjunct. I'm Harry Corbett or Jim Henson. I am Mr Derek. I'm nothing without them – forever an accomplice or assistant to the non-human stars.

And more than happy with that.

Monday 7 June
Back in Scotland for a photoshoot with a statue.

While that sounds thrilling enough in itself, I again tried to make this trip north even more worth my while by heading up a hill yesterday – Beinn Bhuidhe, an isolated western outlier of those shapely peaks known as the Arrochar Alps, which lie no more than forty minutes or so from Glasgow. Olive and Mabel found the expedition a good deal easier than either me or my brother Colin, who had come along for the day out – although at one point Olive did start limping, but since it was at the end of the long, flat walk-in and just before we started heading sharply uphill, I accused her of being dramatic. A quick study of leg and paw revealed nothing and after the award of some medicinal cheese she had clearly forgotten which leg was supposed to be sore. Thereafter she galloped up the steep, heathery slopes and, at the summit, each dog was able to add another Munro and yet more mild cheddar to their personal collection.

This morning we are taking things far more gently, in Alloway, in my home county of Ayrshire, merely posing for pictures at the sculpture of two dogs – the 'Twa Dogs' of the poem by Robert Burns. With his unofficial status as the national poet of Scotland, but also known around the world, this area – centred on the nearby cottage where he spent his early years – is a major tourist attraction.

I applaud their thinking in having two quite well-recognised modern dogs to help publicise the recently completed piece of art. In fact, initially I had been told that I was surplus to requirements as they were only expecting the dogs – a decision which I considered harsh but fair. However, I explained that I would have to come along anyway since neither Olive nor Mabel have an Uber account and I might also be useful in getting them to behave themselves. Although before long, the artistic ambitions of the photographer collide with the independently creative minds of the dogs and while Olive does dutifully replicate the pose of one of the statues, Mabel spends more of her time either licking my face or hoping for a small hug.

I suspect that dogs were altogether hardier in the

late-eighteenth century, when the poem which inspired the sculpture was written. It involves the two characters of the title – canine friends Caesar and Luath,* who belong to rich and poor man respectively – sitting down after their frolics one day to chat about the inequalities and injustices of the human world.

The dogs have none of the vices or vanities of mankind and eventually Luath, the collie belonging to the peasant farmer (often referred to as a cotter, by Burns – I know where I come from) explains to Caesar that his poor owner is actually happier with his lot than the rich, as the most important things to him are simply relaxing in the bosom of his loving family after a hard day's work. A family which he obviously hasn't spent months with in lockdown. But, as they end their chat, both dogs are very certain of one thing – that they are fortunate to be well removed from the strange and unpleasant ways of the human world:

> 'When up they gat an' shook their lugs,
> Rejoic'd they werena men but dogs'

---

* Luath (Gaelic for 'swift' or 'nimble') was in fact the name of Burns' own beloved collie – the two of them said to be inseparable and the dog often at his feet when writing. According to a record left by Burns' brother Gilbert, Luath was killed on the eve of their father's death by 'the wanton cruelty of some person' and Burns wrote 'The Twa Dogs' as tribute to his companion. There are various statues dedicated to the bard and his dog around the world, including a particularly fine one in Winthrop Square in Boston. Like Boatswain, Luath lives on.

Having finished with the photoshoot – Olive and Mabel eventually delivering well by sharing a bench and various poses alongside the bronze Caesar and Luath – I drive us all back down the road. Four long hours are spent in the car, including a forty-five minute traffic jam with my back seizing up and a small vein in my temple starting to twitch and when we finally arrive, I open the boot where the twa dogs have been sleeping, stretched out in great comfort and lightly drooling on a rug. So, gently awakened, they hop down and contemplate their schedule for the remainder of the day: food, possibly followed by a nice walk and then, if they can fit it in between biscuits, another snooze. Meanwhile, I remove my case and struggle with the paraphernalia of toys, leads and beds and look forward to an evening of doing my VAT return. I can only watch with envy as they head inside – shaking their ears and rejoicing as they go.

Thursday 10 June

Even after six months or so, we are still getting used to the different walks available in a new area. This morning we spent an hour or so collectively investigating aromas and eating shrubs alongside a nearby trail, although I was more overseeing these proceedings than playing an active part. It was on one of those very useful paths fashioned from a disused railway line – the only disappointment in this type of walk coming when I make the decision to turn round and both Olive and Mabel suggest that they would rather carry on, as heading back where we have already been, past things already sniffed, is a monumental waste of their time.

When we do get back to the car, I begin the painstaking process of trying to dry Mabel and clean mud from Olive – with both in a state of profound melancholy that it is all over – when a woman shouts across the car park, 'YOU DID ONLINE DATING WITH YOUR DOGS!' And I very quickly rush across to say hello, but also partly to try and quieten her with other people now staring.

Later in the morning, back at home, those of us who are physically capable turn our gaze upwards as we are promised the heavenly glory of a partial solar eclipse, with the moon passing across a portion of the sun. It's quite a rare event – the next partial eclipse seen in the UK will be in autumn 2022. As for the next total eclipse – well, that will be on 23 September 2090 and Mabel, in her endlessly optimistic way, has kept the day clear in her diary.

I pay close attention to the oft-given warning not to stare directly at the eclipse for fear of scorching one's retinas, which might well end in another trip to the optician where I'll be reminded that I'm in the early stages of decrepitude. As it happens, I do my eyes no harm at all by staring directly at a grey layer of cloud which, when we reach the wondrous moment of peak eclipse, changes by a tiny and imperceptible fraction of greyness. Even solar eclipses are dull at the moment.

As I head back inside, I see that Simon next door has a new lawnmower. This once would have been an equally dull sight to me and yet I stand, admiring its shape and colours for a while as if gazing at the awesome majesty of a solar corona, before realising that middle age has now fully claimed me. It's not necessarily a cheering thought, but it's unavoidable. It's just something that happens while you're not paying attention.

Friday 11 June

Second vaccination today – this one administered in a chemist's, rather than the car park of a hotel. No queue, no fuss and the process lasting about three minutes in total. Miraculous how easy it all is now. Yet this situation we are in, and our perceived scientific pathway out of it, still has a tendency to show us some of the worst of people.

A Brazilian physician, it appears, is offering a full supply of Covid medications online, which sounds thoroughly generous and most helpful – in particular in that country where the situation is so grave – but the medicines he provides are in fact those used to combat lice and, what's more, to receive them you have to subscribe to his YouTube or Instagram channels. Shysters with added vanity and neediness... Amidst the outrage I sign up on behalf of Olive and Mabel.

Inducement is taking place in the United States as well, but in the opposite direction, as in certain areas they appear to have a surplus of vaccines and a deficit of people who are keen to make use of it. As they approach saturation point of the willing, in large swathes of the country the powers that be are now reduced to offering a variety of bribes. In some states they will gift you free beer with a vaccination – something I wasn't offered at Boots. Residents in West Virginia are being lured in very West Virginian fashion with a chance to win trucks, hunting rifles and shotguns. One company has offered a free doughnut every single day for a year if you can provide proof of vaccination – effectively saying, 'I don't like the sound of this Covid, but Type 2 diabetes? Now *that's* the disease for me…'

I cannot stress how familiar this all seems to a dog owner, with the memory of several occasions where pills have had to be painstakingly stuffed into a piece of cheese, or perhaps wrapped in a concealing cloak of bacon and hidden deep within the rest of their food. Then, watching with enormous satisfaction as everything is wolfed down and yet afterwards, like some performance of street magic, the pill is left lying in the bowl, worked free by sleight of tongue – the dog in question looking up and saying, 'Don't try this shit again, Andrew.' Of course, this was all in dog days long before Olive came along – if any medication has to be taken orally by her, then you just place it on top of her kibble and she considers it a pleasant garnish. Or you simply drop it on the floor and tap a foot by it.

So perhaps that is the answer – rather than exchange doughnuts for proof of vaccination, you have it in pill form secreted in the depths of the sugar-glazed goodness which is then sold to unsuspecting customers. It could be said for that method to work, those unvaccinated would have to be more dense than your average canine. I will let others be the judge.

Much of our evening of celebration at being better protected against a virus – or injected with the spawn of Satan, depending on your point of view – is spent administering our own preventative treatment to Mabel. A tick approximately the size of a tennis ball has burrowed into the rolls of her neck and comprehensive proof is given that dogs feel almost no pain in this area, since we spend about half an hour trying to dig it out with ever-decreasing subtlety until eventually I am hacking away as if mining for coal. In the end we remove only part of it, which is far from an ideal result but Mabel enjoyed being the centre of attention for a while and there was no need for a biscuit as compensation. Although both received one anyway.

Sunday 13 June

For the first time this year, it's hot, or at least by the low standards of these parts. And by the even lower standards of our dogs, with Olive in particular considering anything beyond fifteen degrees rather balmy. It takes little more than that for her to begin panting away and since this produces the effect of her laughing, I decide to use her as a test-audience for some of my new material with her appreciative reaction giving me a confidence boost. The other symptom shown by Olive when the mercury rises is that she enters a semi-catatonic state, moving around at such a lethargic pace that you imagine what you are seeing is actually a super slo-mo replay of something which happened moments before.

Yet at the same time, the deeply confusing dog brain is at work within both Olive and Mabel whereby they are drawn, lizard-like, to the sun, flinging themselves onto the hot paving stones in the full glare to sear themselves on either side.

I do understand that their fur, which is such good winter insulation, is also pretty effective at regulating temperature, providing a cushion of air between the layers. The problem is the areas with less coverage – the skin of Mabel's underside in particular – takes on a rather pink hue. After about ten minutes or so they make the scientific breakthrough of discovering that the sun is hot and that, as a result, they are also hot, so they head inside or find some shade. Ten minutes later they return because they'd quite like to be hot again.

I decide that I should try to help them out. This being a fundamental mistake since no help which I offer the dogs has ever been accepted – they always have to come to something from the viewpoint that it has been their idea. My assistance in the past in lifting them into cars has only ever been met with a struggle of flailing legs until they feel firm ground beneath their paws again. Or my offer to remove a bit of stick from between their teeth which is causing them great discomfort is accepted only after a period of firm resistance.

Nevertheless I resurrect the long-abandoned film prop of the paddling pool, dragging it out of the garage and filling it from the tap outside. Olive and Mabel edge closer, heads tilted and transfixed by my ability to summon the elemental forces of nature at will. Since both of them love water and very much need to cool off, it seems a no-brainer to me. Unfortunately a no-brainer will often defeat, or at the very least earn a goalless draw with these dogs and they stand, panting in the heat, desperate to somehow lower their temperature, gazing into the gently rippling pool and wondering what the solution to their great conundrum might possibly be. I make encouraging noises with no progress, so tenderly lift one of Olive's front paws and place it in the water – at which point she reacts as if electrocuted and reverses at a frantic pace, showing her first turn of speed of the day. Then lovely, wise Mabel comes tentatively forward, examines the pool and its contents before starting to lap gently at the water. Not exactly what I was looking for, but I suppose it all helps.

Monday 14 June

Agoraphobia / **ægərəˈfəʊbiə** / *noun*
late 19th cent: from Greek, *agora* 'place of assembly,
marketplace'

Quite what was so terrifying about the agora – the
meeting place of ancient Greece – I'm not sure. Perhaps
it was that you might be enjoying a seemingly harmless conversation before having your point of view
thoroughly dismantled by Socratic elenchus. Or that
you could be approached by any number of people
with clipboards hoping you'll take part in a survey on
the government's much-criticised plans to build a giant
wooden horse.

But whatever it was, the modern-world anxiety which
carries its name is real. I wouldn't presume to have the
fear itself, more a deep discomfort. I am the man who
has business to attend to in the agora but really rather
wouldn't. I am Pheidippides, dutifully shouting news
of sporting battles, but only if Pheidippides longed all
the while to be wandering with his dogs through the
Pangaion Hills.

I'm in London for a week, covering the tennis at the
Queen's Club, and the city is alive again. Which is a
mightily good thing, of course, after all we have been
through. It is busy and it is loud. It is whirring around
in a way that big cities do.

There are people here, which probably shouldn't come as too much of a surprise. But there appear to be far more of them, people who were missing the last time I was here, still confined to quarters. Those who are enjoying the weather and their own release and the fact that many of the more palatable aspects of life are returning. And, with the re-emergence of people, comes traffic once more. Although a transformation does seem to be taking place in London and the cars are almost outnumbered by the smaller vehicles – dozens of commuters hurtling around on electric scooters, racing the delivery riders who skip happily through lights and onto pavements in the urgent transport of a rapidly cooling burger and warming salad.

But yes, there are people. It shouldn't feel remarkable, yet does. There are people in bars and in restaurants. There are people chatting and laughing and arguing, or pausing to lean on the edge of Putney Bridge and watch the sun setting beyond the boathouses. There is music floating out of open windows or making a more brief, intrusive appearance from a passing convertible driven by a tool. The sounds all blend together in the symphony of city noise – sharp, staccato horns above the bass rattle of a diesel bus, sirens on police cars which rise and fall as they race through the streets. And the exquisite solo of a man who declares his intention to do me some damage because I am walking on the pavement and don't immediately leap out of the way of his bike. All life is here. All is more as it should be – or at least more as you would expect it to be. The senses overload in a city on a warm summer night.

Having returned, happily undamaged, to my accommodation for the week, I remember one other sensation of London in the summer. It is hot. Not, of course, in the way that you would find in a metropolis of warmer climes, but there they have invested in means to combat the heat. London is somewhere on a par with the ancient Greek city states in terms of air-conditioning development. In our country of narrow meteorological extremes there is no real point in making preparations for anything too far from the average. So we don't and instead we talk about how extraordinary it all is – weather forever taking us by surprise.

It is, of course, far more environmentally friendly that we are left in a natural state but, to counter that, this evening I appear to be turning into a fossil fuel myself, thus negating any ecological benefits. I lie on top of the covers, all windows open, which allows the warm air of the night outside to come in and mingle with the hot air of the room. This does at least start to get the new blend of warm-to-hot air moving around, but the price I pay is that it also admits the noise of the street – predominantly the revving and the chatter from the moped riders at the takeaway below. I catch only the crescendos of their conversation but they seem to be discussing if they might one day get round to sitting their driving tests.

And I lie sweltering within, dreaming of mountain snow. Not even a child's paddling pool to help.

I am also thinking of this readjustment for me, and one being made by all of us – a return to the way we used to be. And I can't escape the uncomfortable truth that part of me has been happy during the past year and even amidst various stages of lockdown – because some of what has happened has been enjoyable. Of course, I want to get back to normality, or as much of its twisted remains that we can salvage, but you do become institutionalised and there is a comfort in staying in the womb.

We have all been in some sort of prison, but if you have been in there for long enough it can be difficult on release. When you have lived a closed life of rules and regulations, tightly ordered and controlled and you emerge, blinking into the light with all suddenly busy and chaotic by comparison, then of course it will be daunting.

And if you not only felt safe in that prison, but saw out your time in relative comfort or had some success there, then it is natural to feel a reluctance to leave the incarceration behind. The caged bird who, when the door is opened, takes one uncertain look outside and returns to nibbling on a lovely bit of millet. The inmate who flings his holdall over his shoulder and walks with trepidation towards the bus stop, glancing back at the barbed wire and towering walls, where he ran a flourishing porn and cigarette business and became table tennis champion of D-Block.

I also fear that after living for a while in a sanitised environment, with little exposure to germs and microbes, I now have an immune system on a level with those Amazonian tribes who had never met anybody from the outside world and were devastated by loggers with measles or a missionary with a slight cold. Hearing a coughing fit is now enough to turn your head and I contemplate a system whereby there is a mandatory requirement for hay-fever sufferers to wear a T-shirt or baseball cap with the inscription 'IT'S NOT WHAT YOU THINK'.

So it is that I view other people with some suspicion and judgement. Even though I am well aware that every one of them has their own story; every one is a person in much the same place, trying to get through the same situation as best they can. They are each just happy to be emerging from all that has happened, but still I drift around with my hackles as high as Mabel when she thinks she is in danger of being molested by a passing schnauzer.

And yet, if you are otherwise strong and in good health, you cannot shut yourself off from the world – taking a Howard Hughes approach by renting out a hotel penthouse, closing the blinds and adopting a casual attitude to personal grooming. I am well aware that I am not made for summer in a city – or any season – and Samuel Johnson's theory doesn't work for everyone as it is actually the life of London that makes me tired.

But sometimes you have no choice. Or rather the choice you have made forces it upon you and you have to return to a busier world. Humans are social creatures. Even those who claim otherwise really cannot hide away, withdrawn forever in a safe and comfortable place. It might be easy, but it's not healthy. So I know it is time to once again walk down a pavement, to get the underground, to politely decline offers of physical harm and to try and ease my way through crowds of fellow people. It's time to walk once again through the bustling and noisy agora.

Tuesday 15 June

It turns out there has been no baby boom as a result of lockdown. It was initially believed that there could be a surge in births around a year after we were all closed up indoors, as if boredom would compel us to think of other pursuits beyond playing Scrabble, or that the whole thing might be fun and create the romantic atmosphere of a long weekend in a ski chalet. In fact, the birth rate has dropped and the divorce rate has rocketed. Perhaps it is not the virus itself which will end the human race, rather a steadily falling population caused by household arguments and strategic headaches.

So I turn my attention to a more comforting story in the news this morning of a dog called Lol, who lives and works in Cahors, south-west France. I say works, because Lol is an official victim support dog in the courtroom in the town. Being a black Labrador (naturally) he already has the robed, judicial look and is available during hearings, often involving the psychological as well as physical damage of domestic abuse. If the prosecutor decides that the victims in a particular case would benefit, Lol is summoned to help move things along with his soothing presence or by the employment of more advanced skills since he has been trained to nuzzle up to victims. In one case mentioned, an elderly couple who had been deeply traumatised by a violent burglary were only able to testify with Lol close at hand, making full use of his postgraduate diploma in gentle leaning.

'The crucial thing is that the dog doesn't judge you,' says the head of the bar association for the area – which is fortunate, since with a Labrador, everybody would be acquitted. It's also fortunate that neither Olive nor Mabel have been put to work in such an environment. Mabel would cause frequent adjournments as she arrived late and nervous, with her briefcase falling open to reveal only a stuffed owl. Olive could be very easily bribed by any of the accused.

The final item of news to pique my interest today doesn't make the papers, but emerges from home, that Simon's new mower has exploded on its first use. The lessons learned are not to covet thy neighbour's mower and also that looks are not everything. I imagine him sitting now, face charred and hair askew, recovering from the trauma – with Dexter nearby, offering all the psychological support he can muster.

Wednesday 16 June

Still in London, but feeling odd.

Low.

Everybody has good days and bad days – more so now than ever. The question is how do you deal with it and what do you say?

Probably nothing, because you also know that you really have no reason to feel that way.

Or you tell those people closest to you. Perhaps even mention it late at night to your dogs to get it off your chest. Maybe just tell them with a stroke of a domed head, or by gently working a folded, soft ear between thumb and forefinger and using them as a living, breathing, sleeping stress ball.

Sometimes you tell nobody. And those small furry counsellors are far away. So in the end you talk only inwardly...tell yourself that you are fed and you are comfortable and you are safe.

And trust that it will pass.

Thursday 24 June

I spent a good few minutes crawling around on the grass today, staring at a moth.

It was an interlude during part of my wider ongoing plan to try and soften the troubles of the world through gardening. Anger and anxiety soothed by weeding appears to be the way forward. Although, as my education in horticultural matters continues, my toughening up in terms of the natural world remains a far slower work in progress.

Hence the moth-staring, as I appeared to have grievously injured one while cutting the grass. Subsequent investigations have revealed that it was a Large Yellow Underwing and since they are nocturnal fliers, I realise that it was probably snoozing gently in some undergrowth after its nightshift when the mower crashed through the roof and did the damage. So I watched it hobbling across the lawn, with one wing broken and I wondered about fashioning some sort of tiny moth splint. Then I admitted to myself that it was probably not long for this world and just let it continue to move towards a final resting place in the flowers on the far side – taking some comfort from the fact that with the grass now very short indeed it was at least making good time.

I really must become more hardened to the ways of the world, as this moth concern is not an isolated incident. The lawn has recently become covered by a carpet of clover. On the plus side, my knowledge of the plant is growing as quickly as the clover itself – there is white clover (also known as Dutch clover) and red clover, which is apparently the national flower of Denmark (and is really more purple). But all of this clover knowledge is far less relevant than the fact that the bees are very fond of both types and are currently massing in their hundreds to gather what pollen they can. As a result, the cutting of grass has become a lengthy exercise since I slam on the brakes every time it appears that I am going to decapitate one of them. Instead I cough politely and gently nudge them with the front wheels, or even wait until they have filled their six boots, taken on board all that they require and flown off.

Not that the bees are singled out for any special treatment. Today, when approaching a thick tuft of longer, damp grass with the strimmer, a small frog flung itself clear of the spinning wire at the last second. If he – or she, it was hard to tell from a distance – hadn't done so and I had witnessed the mangling I don't really know how I would have coped. Probably by sending an enormous bouquet of flowers to the family and agreeing to say a few words at the funeral.

I'm well aware of how oversensitive I am to the lives or plights of animals. That I mourn a snail which I have stepped on with a telling crunch in the dark. That I can't pass a transporter full of livestock without a cloud of sadness sitting over me for the rest of the journey. That it is perhaps odd for me to consider driving into oncoming traffic at high speed to avoid a collision with a pheasant – happier that I had done it no harm and ready to use the dimness of the bird as a mitigating factor on my insurance claim. And how strange it is to be tortured by the slightest accidental wounding of an animal, to the extent that I am ceding the right of way to insects and minor amphibians when cutting the grass.

Yet to me it is even more strange to possess the biblical idea that we have dominion over all other creatures – that we are superior in our rights merely because of superiority in brain function. That advantage should only give us the responsibility to look after all others, not the right to do with them as we please. Other creatures are almost all dependent for their survival, either individually or collectively, on what we – simply the most intelligent of the animals – choose to do and how we choose to live.

Of course I do realise something of a flaw in the argument that no harm of another lifeform should ever be tolerated, as various members of the animal world spend large parts of their lives either eating each other or planning how best to make that happen. But, there, the harm is necessary rather than the collateral damage of garden maintenance or, worse still, hunting for the pleasure of it. In the animal world they are all just doing what they can to survive.

And yet I will still try to pretend that even that doesn't occur. Whenever I watch a nature documentary, I swiftly hop to another channel as the cheetah closes in on the gazelle. Then I can play out the rest of the scene in my head where that gazelle had skipped happily away to live a long and prosperous life, finally departing only because of a heart attack sometime in its early sixties during vigorous lovemaking. I still bear the mental scars from one documentary I saw where a killer whale caught an unsuspecting seal and, to ease my discomfort, Caroline said, 'Don't worry, it will all have been over very quickly.' This was immediately followed by the gentle tones of David Attenborough explaining, 'The mother and her calf will play with their prize for some time' as whale and offspring tossed the not yet expired creature between each other like a beach ball.

Those who make these documentaries know the truth and they know that the natural world is not that of Disney – and those of us who anthropomorphise it or want every thing within it to live in harmony are deluded. Never intervene, is the first rule of those film crews capturing the wild. The savagery of nature, red in tooth and claw; the stark truth of it must be left to play out unaltered. Therefore I would be thrown off the crew on the first day, after racing out from our hidden position to slap a python as it closed in on a raccoon. Or, on seeing an approaching crocodile, shouted warnings to the one or two water buffalo who were having a chat and looking the other way. And besides, what if an eagle were to swoop down on the python? Do I slap that predator away as well? Or if the raccoon itself bears down on a rodent or two? I can't go around slapping animals all day long – I just haven't got the time. I should probably accept that it is simply the natural way of things.

Once more, however, my odd thought process leads me to bring Olive and Mabel out of semi-retirement, deciding to make a nature documentary of my own. What's more, the dogs don't actually have to do anything for this one, since the action happened a couple of weeks ago on a walk. Mabel performing her ridiculous stalking of Olive – a master of stealth and cunning only in her own head – before launching herself at her profoundly untroubled friend.

Here too, I was tempted to intervene – not to save the prey from harm, but to prevent Mabel from embarrassing herself any further. But I let it unfold as nature intended and all I have to do now is find some dramatic music and appropriate words, delivered in the style of a wildlife documentary.

I realise that with the release of the video, *National Geographic* are now unlikely to come calling when they need a narrator and that I have probably lost any chance to do the job seriously. But it's surely for the best anyway. Nobody really wants to hear Attenborough's successor solemnly intoning…

'With the long Antarctic winter approaching, the penguins must eat as much as…SHIT, there's a leopard seal! *Swim* little penguin… For Christ's sake, SWIM…'

Sunday 27 June

A lot of people are keeping a very keen eye on the traffic lights just now – the system whereby we are informed which countries we might be able to travel to or, more pertinently, return from.

Green – No quarantine necessary on arrival back in the UK.

Amber – Unless fully vaccinated, ten days of quarantine at home.

Red – Ten days of quarantine in an official hotel.

It can be deeply frustrating as countries might switch quickly and without any real warning between the colours. There is always the chance that your holiday in Mexico might now be a day-trip, or will be followed by an additional staycation in a small hotel room at Gatwick Airport.

Again, dogs should allow themselves a quiet chuckle at all of this, since these are the kind of regulations that they have had to follow for decades. When I was growing up it was made clear that the reason we didn't take our pets if we went on holiday abroad was that they would have to spend six months in a German or Italian kennel. This greatly troubled my young mind as I couldn't bear to be without them for that long and, furthermore, I knew that our dogs spoke neither of those languages – and our cat, Ludwig, no more than very basic German but not really enough to get by. I was also filled with horror stories about rabies being rife among the wild and uncivilised dogs of the Continent – to the extent that I remember fleeing, terrified, out of a café in Florence where I had been enjoying my pistachio ice cream, convinced that a dog hurtling towards our table was foaming at the mouth, when really it had just had a drink of water and was now coming over to say hello.

Then pet passports came in and with them the ability to prove that your dog had had a vaccination or medication against all manner of canine plagues. Throwing in the additional security of microchips and dogs can now travel far and wide, although they may need to be blood-tested if returning from a country that is not listed. And if not adhering to any of those rules, dogs can still expect a four-month stay in a government-appointed kennel. So all we have done now is join them in their world of strictly controlled travel, with many of us complaining that this is unjust and a restriction on freedom and our rights. Although I'm not sure why we feel that we deserve special treatment.

As it happens, today I am getting ready to travel as well, but only in the car and only a few hours down to London for Wimbledon, which begins tomorrow and is resolutely on the green list. And yet I will be away for a fortnight – the longest spell away from Olive and Mabel in quite some time and at least two of us are taking it badly.

For all that I mock our dogs and their apparent lack of intelligence, there is clearly deep, long-term memory, as Olive obviously remembers the process of me leaving to go on a trip. While I do my packing, she comes and sits by the bed – tail down, ears plastered to the side of her head and, as I place clothes in the case, she doesn't take her eyes off me. I know that she understands these suitcases and what they mean.

So I chat away and then sit down beside her, stroking her head and telling her that yes, I am going somewhere else for a while and that yes, I will miss her very much, but I will come back. To which she offers the very gentle, thoughtful stare into the distance that Labradors can produce, as if pondering the notion. Although in truth it is more likely that she is fondly remembering the time a small piece of ham fell onto the kitchen floor.

As I head out to the car, leaving both dogs at the back door, Olive looks rather sorrowful while the less comprehending Mabel is once more simply wagging her tail to such an extent that she might soon fall over. But I take comfort from the fact that it will be no more than a few minutes before they have moved on and will be thinking only about their evening snack and snooze routine. I wish I could move on quite so easily.

Monday 28 June

London.

It is now cool and damp here and strangely warm and sunny further north – the weather is out of kilter. Yet not quite as imbalanced as in Canada where I see that it has reached fifty degrees. Fifty degrees Celsius. Something, you feel, is very wrong.

At the rather chillier Wimbledon, there is no real time

to ease myself into proceedings as on this, the first day, I am hurled into the deep end on Centre Court, commentating on Novak Djokovic against the young British wildcard Jack Draper – and doing so in the company of John McEnroe.

McEnroe, one of the greats of the game and a quite brilliant commentator, is also a reasonably intimidating figure and small talk never appears to be high on his agenda with those who are not within his very closest inner circle. Fortunately I have a well-practised technique for dealing with this, which is to agree with absolutely everything he says. I've done it for over ten years and this unequal and possibly grovelling relationship seems to work. Although there is still a very good chance he thinks my name is Adam.

As it happens, his level of expertise means that he is almost always right in any case. And so we plod along in this fashion where I simply hope to alight upon a nice turn of phrase or the right exclamation to go with a certain passage of play. All the while half expecting him to snap and call me an imbecile. At which point I would say, 'Couldn't agree more, John…' while nodding enthusiastically.

Yet the commentary passes well enough and the match throws up plenty to discuss, which always brings the very best out of my illustrious co-commentator. I even feel bold enough to venture an opinion or two of my own, but still managing to lose confidence halfway through the sentence and so adding a questioning intonation as a get-out clause should it prove to be thoroughly incorrect.

'Certainly looks to be receiving a bit too deep…on… second…serrrrve…?'

'That is exactly right, Andrew,' says John. And my heart fills with joy.

In the evening I lie awake again, sleep not coming easily with music arriving from neighbouring flats but also the strange, anxious, almost human-sounding calls of urban foxes nearby. I imagine they are either gleefully dragging a torn bin bag around and rifling through the contents, or they are two joined together post-coitus in the rather bizarre fox manner and are now shouting their surprise at the situation.

Whatever the reason, I abandon designs on sleep and head to make a cup of tea and switch on the television, which doesn't appear to be working, so instead take an idle stroll through social media. In the past I have had a habit of deactivating Twitter entirely during sporting events that I am working on, but I feel that my following now is more dog-based, so have left it alone. As it is, every single message seems to be on the same harmless theme.

'You talking about sport doesn't feel right. Could we have Olive and Mabel as ball girls?'

I know I have brought this on myself and duly accept my fate.

Wednesday 30 June

Still talking about sport today rather than dogs and I find myself scheduled to commentate on Andy Murray's second-round match at Wimbledon – the preparation for which takes me down a familiar, if slightly baffling path.

Murray has announced on social media a venture into the mysterious world of our non-fungible token friends, or NFTs. In a couple of days' time there will be an auction, carried out in conjunction with Wimbledon as well as a new NFT trading company, where you can buy the actual moment he won the men's singles title for the first time in 2013. How this is possible I'm not entirely sure. But one person most certainly is sure and that's Beeple, since he has founded the company in question as he looks for ways to spend his $69 million beyond buying a large yacht or a small country. Apparently NFTs have taken a bit of a dive since the start of the year and are now worth about a tenth of their former value. And while I still don't pretend to be fully on top of any of this subject, I'm sure that this is not good.

Beeple's company describes itself as 'the memory palace of the metaverse'. And further explanation is given that the metaverse is the universe of the virtual worlds that are all connected. Their aim is to 'immortalise iconic moments from history on blockchain' and Murray's debut victory at Wimbledon is their very first sale. And I'm glad I've been able to clear that up for you.

As examples, we could try and publish photos of

some of those iconic moments in this book, but since they are shortly to be owned by somebody who will have their absolute ownership logged on something called an Ethereum blockchain, it would no doubt cost us dearly in an online lawsuit with a virtual lawyer. Perhaps one who arrives at the hearing in the form of a slightly worried talking cat.

Despite my bafflement, I suspect that this is just another example of the future digital world – an idea which might seem strange now, but will develop into something entirely commonplace. Consequently, my grappling to comprehend all of this will age very badly and in thirty years' time will seem, to the people of 2050, like my great aunt once appeared to me as I tried to explain the concept of email.

The most important thing to point out is that this diversion into the memory palace of the metaverse has taken up a considerable amount of my time in the actual-verse this morning – time that should have been spent on more relevant commentary notes. And I always need to feel that I have done more than enough to give me a wide selection of talking points during a match – ammunition enough to carry you through the broadcast. Because quite often when I commentate on big occasions, I find myself coming down with a mild outbreak of impostor syndrome.

This is not something as malevolent as doubt, as I am confident enough in my broadcasting abilities, but rather the sensation that none of this is really meant to be happening. Or at the very least that it is strange that it *is* happening. A feeling that, even though you have been doing the job for a couple of decades, you have simply been getting away with it all this time and that any moment will come the knock at the door, with some kindly but apologetic representative of the human resources department explaining that there has been a clerical error. And so you are accompanied to the exit – not altogether happy, but accepting it, as you were realistic enough to know this day of reckoning would eventually come.

I suppose it is something that many people must feel about their jobs from time to time. How many of us are entirely on top of the situation and in control throughout? And how many others know that they are largely making it up as they go along – finding their way through life by a combination of bluff and bluster? I'm not suggesting that I am in the group containing the full-on pretenders, as I do believe that I have whatever vague talents are necessary. But at the same time I am well aware of the good fortune that you have to enjoy to find yourself in this position.

Putting such thoughts to one side, I continue my pre-match studies on Murray's opponent – a German called Oscar Otte, who has come through qualifying and is one of the lesser lights of the tennis scene. A fair amount of useful prep for commentary these days can be done by looking at the players' social media feeds – in particular if you are involved with one of the less-heralded players. There you can see photos of a player with their coach or their partner, or at their training base or, as it appears with Otte, a number of pictures of him accompanied by a cockapoo called Hank. I also notice that the player's Instagram bio reads *Dog is God spelled backwards* and while I'm sure my objectivity will not be swayed by his worshipping at the canine church, my suspicion about cockapoos taking over the world grows ever stronger.

Thankfully, when I do pick up the microphone, I successfully manage to avoid mentioning dogs at any point throughout what develops into an absorbing match. Although at one stage, as Murray begins his fightback from two sets to one down, I feel myself about to use the words 'still believing...' but stop just in time as I had used it to describe Mabel hoping to steal a rubber bone from Olive all those months ago.

Yet here, I am being firmly reminded of what a wonderful thing sport involving actual humans can be, as it all finishes with a late-night Murray victory under the roof and lights of Centre Court. How much it helps also to have a live crowd to offer the additional soundtrack. How invested we all become in what is unfolding and how we forget everything else for that time.

When I eventually get back to the apartment, it's well after midnight. The events of the evening are now sitting in my own memory palace of the metaverse – taking their place alongside other memories that shine brightly and many more that gather dust in deeper, more dimly lit rooms – but all remaining entirely under my ownership and able to be recalled whenever I choose. What a strange but privileged job, I think, in this odd world of ours – as I listen again to the foxes nearby, once more enjoying their own historic moment.

JULY 2021

Friday 2 July

Wimbledon does things in its own unique way. Behind the ornate wrought-iron gates of the All England Club, it is of the world but somehow separate from it, almost self-governing under a different constitution and laws – with very specific standards of behaviour and quirks of tradition.

Waiting to commentate on a match today, I am press-ganged into a group of four to go and meet Kate Middleton, a.k.a. Catherine, Duchess of Cambridge – apparently this is an occasional requirement whereby people are offered up to the highest level of special guests, to engage with them in gentle conversation when there is a spare few minutes in the schedule. It is a known fact that she is a dog lover, although whether this extends to knowledge of Olive and Mabel I'm not sure. But I see no reason why she shouldn't settle down with William and the gang of an evening and chuckle at YouTube videos like the rest of us, or perhaps pass round occasional clips on the royal WhatsApp group.

So I am escorted up to the dining room behind the Royal Box on Centre Court, trailing after three greats of the women's game in Tracy Austin, Chris Evert and Pam Shriver. I can't help feeling that I am the odd one out, but I am told that I am simply there to provide interesting and entertaining chat as somebody is under the misguided notion that this is one of my abilities. Perhaps this is what my role in life will be from now on – as the comic relief for assorted dignitaries. Juggling at Brexit talks or rolled out during the interval of a US/China nuclear summit to lighten the mood with a couple of witty stories about a Jack Russell.

Here though, the mood doesn't noticeably require any increase in levity as everybody seems to laugh a lot in the presence of the duchess. She arrives, smiling and very pleasant, but never alone, accompanied by high-ranking officials of the club plus a security detail of about half a dozen – not the caricature of heavily muscled celebrity bodyguards with dark suits and sunglasses, but efficient and almost unseen figures who could no doubt escort you swiftly out of the premises and indeed life itself should you make the wrong move. They position themselves at various points of the room – one settling in by my elbow, as they might well have done a check on my social media history and identified me as a mild halfwit, but decide it's best not to take any chances.

Within moments, Kate and the tennis legends are getting on famously, chatting away happily about anything and everything to do with the sport and, since all five of us are wearing the semi-disguise of masks, I wonder if I shouldn't have simply introduced myself as Pete Sampras and bluffed my way through it. Yet after a couple of minutes I become acutely aware that I am the only one not talking and this is now fast developing into the dynamic of every party I've been to since the age of seventeen. Panicking slightly, I consider regaling everyone with the story of how I ran over a moth in the garden, but accept that it might be too much of a left turn in the conversation. So I continue to stand, mute, on the periphery and if the duchess has noticed my presence at all, it must appear to her that I am only there as some sort of competition winner.

But dogs, as always, are the saviour and the common bond, so often providing conversation starters for the socially challenged among us. I therefore decide to contribute by asking Kate about her own dogs, without realising that the only one whose name I can remember had fairly recently departed. I plough on regardless by saying something non-consequential about Labradors, but simultaneously Kate asks Chris Evert a question about Serena Williams and I'm left talking only to myself, so decide the best option from there is to gently fade out mid-sentence and hope that nobody has noticed.

As we five are talking – or rather the others are and I'm contributing by nodding occasionally – it becomes even more crowded around us in the room, as the guests who have been invited to sit in the Royal Box have arrived. The theme for today is people who had a positive effect during lockdown, with a large number of the invitees those who inspired the nation to exercise. So the guests who now buzz around and spill out onto the famous balcony are a lively and enthusiastic collection of characters to say the least.

The duchess and the tennis players have moved out there as well and are having their photo taken, while not too far away, Joe Wicks and Mr Motivator are into the early stages of a joint selfie session that will go on for some time to come. People continue to waltz around Kate, but mostly they just stare from a distance in admiring and deferential fashion and wonder if they dare approach any closer to this fellow human. Without permission they might find it somewhat tricky as the security detail is now keeping an even closer eye on proceedings and are capable of incapacitating a stray influencer without breaking sweat. Sadly, before any of that is required, the duchess is off and her retinue moves stealthily with her as she is taken onto her next carefully planned conversation, very possibly still wondering who that man was who kept trying to talk about dogs.

Free to depart I head downstairs again, without my own ineffective security complement of two Labradors, trained only in the defensive art of licking people into submission. I move outside, somewhere along the way passing through unseen and largely impassable barriers, pondering once more what very curious creatures we are, leaving behind a tightly controlled life of regulations and its own peculiar confinement. And I walk back to the broadcaster's area, slipping unnoticed and untroubled into the crowd, removing my jester's hat as I go.

Monday 5 July

I read with some interest today that the Duchess of Cambridge has been forced into ten days of isolation after coming into close contact with somebody at Wimbledon who subsequently tested positive for Covid. This is the official line – the truth may be that she is keen to avoid any more uncomfortably awkward conversation.

Friday 9 July

A big match to prepare for today, working on the men's semi-final between Novak Djokovic and Denis Shapovalov. A big match and a small room.

The Centre Court commentary box is a tiny place, but this year we have been operating in commentary teams of just two for almost all matches, giving us more space and enabling us to operate within (or without) what passes for being socially distanced. It is only as we get to the latter stages and matches of greater importance that we have employed the occasional team of three. As it is here, when I am joined by both Tim Henman and Boris Becker, but still with the additional precaution of Perspex screens between us. So we sit in shirts and ties, like the host and two guests on *Celebrity Bank Tellers* – another programme that failed to make it past the commissioning editors.

With three involved, it can also get rather crowded in terms of the voices you hear and since I am in no doubt that people would rather listen to the thoughts of the illustrious pair alongside me, I merely surface every now and again with a phrase or a fact to add the punctuation, or to steer them in a certain direction – all the time aware that too much talk is death to a television commentary and that no viewer has ever complained that their experience has been ruined by a broadcaster not saying enough.

The fractured nature of tennis commentary does give you time to think though. And I don't want to give you the idea that I see the world entirely in canine terms now, but in one of my prolonged silences, where I am letting Tim and Boris chat away while hopefully giving the impression of concentrating fully on what is an engrossing match, I look at the blond and dark-haired co-commentators beside me and my mind briefly presents them as Olive and Mabel substitutes. It's actually not far off the mark in terms of their personalities, but I also make a note – *will Wimbledon let me film a dog video in here next year?* This is when I recognise that I have already been away from them for too long. I also think I should really say something as Djokovic has three match points.

I am, of course, making light of it, as the job here does involve a good deal of thought and concentration.

I sit for a moment after it's over with a growing ache in my temple, but the commentary team is coming in for the next match, so I make my way out into the chattering and excited crowd beneath Centre Court. Tim and Boris plough on in front, recognised by many, but using their auras as some sort of force field, scattering people by sheer fame, heads down and setting such a brisk pace that when the recogniser has remarked to their friends who is passing, it is only the vapour trail that remains and I make far slower progress behind, bouncing along through the wake they have created.

Returning late in the evening once again and with my head still pounding, I go out in search of air and decompression. Three months now without running, so I have brought my bike down and I take it out into Richmond Park, knowing the road which loops around it will soon be empty with the gates closing to cars at about nine o'clock. As I set off and climb one of the many hills of this rolling, bucolic landscape within the city, there are still the low remnants of sunlight remaining – just enough to catch a few vivid green flashes which circle around above the treetops and then settle in for the night on their perches among the leaves and branches. These are some of the famous parakeets of London – ring-necked parakeets to be precise – to be found in many of the parks of the capital, but most abundant here in Richmond Park. The tales of how they came to be here, so far from their native homes in Africa or India, are as colourful as the birds themselves. Some believe that their presence can be traced back to a flock being set free after being used in the production of *The African Queen* at nearby Shepperton Studios in 1951.* Others claim that the presence of the parakeets is entirely down to Jimi Hendrix, strolling out of his home in Mayfair at some point in the late sixties and releasing a breeding pair, for reasons best known to himself and whatever he had ingested that morning. But far more likely is that they have simply multiplied over a couple of centuries or more from the many birds brought in as an exotic species, arriving at London's docks, where the entire world passed through.

Soon it's getting dark and I stop to dig out my lights and take a moment to sit on a fallen tree. In the far distance, the London skyline is shimmering white with flickers of warning red on the tallest buildings and I realise that I'm close to where we filmed with Olive and Mabel for American television nine months ago. With the night falling, no cars are here and no people remain, having headed for the gates at dusk, yet other life is all around. Rabbits, now seen as no more than tiny shadows, flit in and out of the bracken or gather in a small group of silhouettes to discuss the events of

---

* Most of the filming of *The African Queen* was, in fact, done in East Africa and was notable for Katherine Hepburn being in a near-constant state of illness from drinking local water, while Humphrey Bogart remained in robust health after devoting himself to alcohol. The curious thing about the film is that you never see a single parakeet.

the day. From the canopy above comes the chatter of the birdlife and occasionally the squawk of one of the parakeets, which I imagine might be trying to sing the openings bars of 'Purple Haze', passed down through the generations. After a few minutes more I spot one or two deer and they emerge from the deeper areas of undergrowth and draw nearer, relaxed and closing in to the point where I could almost reach out and touch a pelt. So I sit and watch and I listen and I think. I also wonder about heading out of the park myself as it's now well after ten o'clock. But there is no real hurry, so I stay a while longer. My head has eased and far off the noise of the city has fallen away. Nothing more now than the sound of the wind, or waves on a distant shore.

Sunday 11 July

There is an unsettling atmosphere in London and its surrounds today. The final day of Wimbledon certainly has a different ambience; with the matches down to just a few remaining finals, there is a quieter feel to the place. Not many spectators are to be found away from the show courts, but still there is a gradually rising tide of crowd noise, coming instead from the road outside the grounds. Soon, police sirens announce the arrival of a van and a few cars to meet a chanting crowd of hundreds who have gathered to express their displeasure at something which they obviously feel very strongly about. It quickly becomes apparent that they are anti-lockdown and anti-vaccine protesters, mustering at the gates and certain in their minds that those two causes can quite happily be brought together in one catch-all protest.

'YOU... You are a DISGRACE,' shouts the leader into his megaphone, face contorted and addressing anybody within his reach, although looking directly at me as I walk by, on my way to get ready for some gentle commentary and occasional mild chuckling over a mixed doubles final.

'You should be ASHAMED of yourselves...' he carries on and I'm struck by the thought that I've heard or read this sentiment before. It's as if social media has come to the real world and, as he continues, the crowd behind him hurls some similar abuse, effectively retweeting their leader's opinion. No more than fifty yards away, inside Centre Court, a different crowd is watching the men's singles final and chants support for their chosen player. Everybody has to have something to get excited about.

It is not just this corner of London where the masses are gathering. In the room where we sit and wait for our turn to broadcast, one screen is showing the men's final here at the tennis, the other a news report which relays events from Leicester Square, as hundreds of England football supporters get up to some high jinks. For a moment, side by side in my vision, there is a smartly suited Tom Cruise applauding a Djokovic winner from the Centre Court seats, while next to him is an England fan who has shoved a lit flare up his backside. And to those who surround the human distress beacon, the effort appears to be generating similar levels of acclaim.

The latter crowd has managed to leave a trail of destruction around the square while a number choose to storm Wembley Stadium as well. The whole day seems to be an outpouring of pent-up emotion, both good and bad, in this summer of release. An explosion of life in all its forms. It has been a somehow fitting end to a fortnight in the capital where you have been able to feel both the urgent need of people to be out and behaving normally, combined with the simmering tension which has people behaving altogether less normally.

In the evening I leave, driving down to the Kent coast to begin a week of golf coverage at the Open Championship. The motorway is near enough deserted with almost everybody shut inside, but now of their own free will watching the football and, as the miles pass by, the glow of London – and all that lies within it – becomes ever more faint behind me, until eventually it disappears from sight and mind.

Sunday 18 July

Long days of work mean little chance for writing or keeping a diary, but in truth there is not a huge amount to report in any case. This week at the Open Championship has passed without drama and with everything feeling as normal as life can be. Or at least as normal as it has in a very long time. Crowds fill the course at St George's, enjoying the sunshine and warm days. People mostly still taking care, but easing back into the ways that they once knew.

Far more troubling is the news from home that the famous orange rubber bone has gone missing. The dog toy that was briefly so coveted by Mabel and subsequently seen by tens of millions of people around the world – and even interpreted as the US election by those who wished to see it that way – has disappeared.

I say disappeared, but I know exactly what will have happened to it and what criminal negligence I would uncover if I were to investigate further: Dog A or Dog B has taken it out into the garden, whereupon they have been distracted by something of great fascination to their noses and so the previous fondness for the bone has evaporated. Said bone will then have been abandoned deep within the foliage where they had been intrigued by the diverting scent and, since the garden is at its fullest growth, will probably reveal itself only as we move into autumn or winter, uncovered as if by a receding of the tide. And there really is no point in doing anything else but waiting – mostly because our dogs can offer no clues to help us narrow down our search. Ask them, 'Where did you last have it?' and they will reply, 'Have what?' or possibly even, 'Sorry, who are you?'

In the interim, Caroline has bought an identical new one – entirely fungible – and I am sent a video of Mabel parading around with it. She is seemingly happy that she has the rubber bone back in her possession, carrying it proudly and showing it to anybody who is interested and also anybody who is not – as if showing off some new jewellery and being none the wiser that it is entirely fake. Olive maintains her deep suspicions.

I'm determined to find the original though – for some reason it has taken on great significance. And besides, I have always had an emotional attachment to even less celebrated items – reluctant to discard particular objects, as if trying to hold onto days gone by. I'm certainly not a hoarder but it's as if keeping them somewhere, even tidied away in a cupboard, will render memories more vivid and somehow aid us in remembrance of the things we have done, or of the people we were. It might be a pair of shoes, or a T-shirt. Or it might even be a cracked and perishing rubber bone, one of thousands physically identical, churned out in a factory in China – now far more precious as a connection to the past. Decluttering to a minimalist state is good for my mind, but some things are far too important to let go.

Tuesday 20 July

> 'Strange to see how a good dinner and feasting reconciles everybody'
>
> DIARY OF SAMUEL PEPYS, 9 November 1665

Birthday. Forty-eight…

I make another dawn trip to the beach at Formby, as the current spell of hot weather means it is the only practical way to properly exercise Olive and Mabel. After about ten in the morning, Olive will animate herself only to trudge out into the garden and collapse in a heap on the flagstones, which will then require us to scrape up her molten shape about ten minutes later and point her in the direction of the water bowl and shade. But at six in the morning, the temperature is still low enough and there is also the additional promise of diversions into the cooling – although worryingly brown – waters of the Irish Sea.

With the summer holidays now fully underway in England, I consider what a wonderful thing it is that everybody is able to get out and, what's more, to be able to go to events which are being staged again around the country. As Mabel whirls around in front of me, skipping happily over the vast and shapely dunes and very keen to show us all the way to the beach, I notice that they have chosen this location to stage the International Litter Festival and it appears that the competition has been hotly contested in all categories. Both dogs stumble happily over cartons, cans and boxes and Olive in particular seems delighted to have this added attraction as she sticks her nose in a discarded container with trace elements of ketchup. They are taking it all in far better humour than me and I focus my attention instead on the smooth, untroubled sand which starts just a few hundred yards from the car park.

Much of the rest of the day is spent going through notes on the impending Olympic Opening Ceremony – a task where deviation again is the arch enemy. Here, an introductory study of a country leads you down many rabbit holes of deeper but utterly irrelevant investigation. Soon you have discovered that the second cousin of a table tennis player from Lithuania collaborated with Stephen Sondheim on *West Side Story* and before you know it an hour has passed watching musicals on YouTube. Since these diversions are themselves interrupted by searches on what sort of custodial sentence you could expect for maiming somebody who leaves a disposable barbecue and empty cans at a beauty spot, I get far less constructive work done than I had planned.

In the evening, we have arranged to join our neighbours for dinner and, as we arrive, one of the hosts seems particularly pleased to see us. Dexter rushes out to offer his welcome and take our coats while also letting everybody know that people are here, which is great and that they seem harmless, the household is in no danger and that nobody should panic as he races around barking and reminding everybody that it's very important to stay calm. He then looks at the closed gate behind us, feeling that we might have forgotten somebody. We haven't – we just wanted to enjoy an hour or two of an evening not dominated by dog flirting, so have left Olive and Mabel behind, listening to Radio 2.

Even though it has been possible now for a while, this

does all still seem new and unfamiliar – indicating how much we had become used to *not* being able to do this sort of thing. Eating, drinking and chatting – putting the world to rights, or as much as we can. Sharing experiences and stories while Dexter lies rather sadly on his side – the evening not quite as he had hoped or imagined – raising his head once or twice to grudgingly accept a treat, but his heart is full of sorrow and his mind is elsewhere.

Eventually we can see him in his misery no longer, so I go to fetch Olive and Mabel and they come tearing round, following the barbecue scents and the trail which leads to food and people – and people with food. Their arrival duly sparks a transformation in Dexter, who leaps up and pretends that he was just in the middle of telling everyone a very funny story and welcomes the ladies to the party. They rush straight past him – Olive to see if she can persuade anybody to part with edibles, Mabel to find any sort of novel toys in the garden.

Olive has no doubt where her best chance lies and makes an immediate beeline for Simon, placing herself expectantly in front of him because a couple of months ago he gave her a chipolata. Floods and earthquakes might come, war could rage around us, and a Labrador will still be fully focused on a person who once gifted them half an ounce of cured meat.

All this rather thwarts the constant efforts of Dexter to make further progress with Olive. Or any progress. His favoured move appears to be jabbing her repeatedly in the side with his nose, as if a persistent admirer at a nightclub, constantly tapping the object of his desire on the shoulder, while talking about his many achievements and his latest car. Olive is meanwhile doing her very best to ignore him, her attention given instead to the food which Simon brings to the table from time to time or the plate of crisps that has been conveniently left at dog height nearby. But Dexter is nothing if not committed and continues his nose-prodding approach, wagging his tail, now moving on to his successful investments and the time he went jet-skiing off Corfu, while never reading the very obvious signals coming from Olive, who eventually snaps and bares her teeth. Dexter is quite taken aback, to the point where he momentarily falls over, but to his credit bounces straight back up, dusts himself down and has a little think about it all for a moment. Before recommencing jabbing her in the side with his nose.

About twenty yards away on the grass, only just visible thanks to her blonde tones in the fast-disappearing light, Mabel is throwing an old burst football around as if it is the finest thing in the whole world. I watch her for a while, but nobody else is particularly interested in her performance. At the nightclub she is dancing on her own to the song that she loves. And is perfectly happy to do so.

Thursday 22 July

Today is almost entirely taken up by the ample task of Olympic preparation. One of the many problems with not being in Tokyo is that there I could entirely focus on the job at hand. Here, there are several distractions, not least a dog or two wandering up during my deep research on 206 countries and requesting attention. I'm just getting stuck into Djibouti by initially doing no more than reminding myself where it actually is and learning the not massively important fact that its Japanese name is Jibuchi – when Mabel appears, tail scattering notes from the table and asking if I might accompany her to the garden to throw a tennis ball around.

The thing which people do not see, or perhaps consider when watching a sporting event, is quite how much research and preparation has to be done by anybody involved in the broadcast. Knowledge gives you confidence. At the very least the confidence to sound as if you might have a vague idea what you're talking about. For a rugby match on a Saturday you will spend a good part of the week preparing; for a ceremony which is largely incomprehensible to those watching without an accompanying voice, it involves as many days as you can spare on the homework. Add in the requirement of finding several interesting things to say about almost every country on Earth and it is all done with a feeling of dread fear as well.

But then again, I do realise that breaks are also very necessary. And besides, what could possibly be more important than spending an idle twenty minutes watching two dogs trying to catch a ball, careering through a flower bed and eventually emerging triumphant from the depths of a hedge, carrying both ball and large elements of undergrowth in their mouths?

Yes, my decision is made. Jibuchi can wait.

Friday 23 July

Of all the broadcasting that I have been involved with over the last twenty years or so, nothing makes me quite so tense or is quite so demanding as the opening ceremony to an Olympic Games. It is four and a half hours of constant concentration and focus – keenly observing what is unfolding on the screen and trying your very best to explain exactly what it all means, while being well aware that you are watching something which is of deep cultural significance and importance to the host country, even if it appears to be simply two people dancing in large hats.

You are always thinking about what is coming up next while making any number of decisions about when to speak and when to let it breathe. And, in the very small windows of opportunity that open, you wonder what to say when you do decide to utter something. There is also the enormous Parade of Nations to consider, when you are forever – and it does seem like forever – treading the fine line between making attempts to be interesting and entertaining enough but also avoiding the possibility of causing offence, leading to social media vilification and a siege of British embassies in at least three or four countries.

My co-commentator Hazel Irvine and I have seen a rehearsal for this one, but a lot of the crucial elements are not revealed until moments before it all gets underway. Understandably, given the background to the Games, this is a particularly low-key ceremony which involves far less technological wizardry or moments of light-hearted entertainment and a good deal more of children singing in harmony and about harmony. Any number of promises are made about the world moving forward as one to a much more wholesome future. Mind you, promises are often made at Olympic Games which return as an empty echo in the years to come. The theme of the ceremony in Rio de Janeiro five years ago was saving the environment and hosting the 'Green Games', since when Brazil has rolled up its sleeves and really got stuck into clearing the Amazon rainforest at a most impressive rate.

And, for all the talk of togetherness and unity tonight, there is clearly a fondness around the world for creating our own smaller units. Drawing lines on maps – putting up borders and pulling up the drawbridge. I resist any temptation to say this and just mention how smiley everybody appears, and look, this is the Suginami Junior Choir...children are the future and really can show us the way.

But, despite the obvious issues elsewhere and

everywhere outside, there is something about the occasion which can affect even the most jaded observer. Those smiles of the athletes in the stadium are genuine and are the same from whichever country they come and whatever their stories might be. No matter how cynical one might be about the Olympics or modern sport, it can succeed in bringing human beings together. Divisions and boundaries (for the most part) slip away and for this time all you are left with are the people. Yes, people who will be trying to beat each other – sometimes literally – in competition, but they will smile before, sometimes during and perhaps for a good while after, having shared an experience.

In fact, I find myself an even more firm believer in the erasing of boundaries and divisions as 206 nations and teams come into the stadium – I am not necessarily advocating dictator-led super-states as the way forward, but it would be helpful in terms of my workload. With fewer athletes present, the countries arrive at a dizzying rate and Hazel and I attempt to say something about each and every one of them: sporting pedigree, main exports, national costume, history of revolution and civil war, as well as Albania's abiding love for the films of Norman Wisdom. Very little is left unsaid.

Then, the very small team from Djibouti arrives and I am temporarily lost for words, so Hazel steps in.

'Djibouti...on the Horn of Africa between Eritrea, Ethiopia and Somalia. With a coastline where the Red

Sea turns into the Gulf of Aden – strategically very important and actually the location of the United States' largest military base on the continent.'

'Mmm... Absolutely, Hazel. Jibuchi... Ah now, here comes Jamaica...' I continue, while inwardly promising to have a stern chat with Mabel when I get home.

Tuesday 27 July

Walking through the drizzle in Salford today and my mind drifts elsewhere. It often does.

I remember, while staying in Tokyo during the Rugby World Cup two years ago, taking a stroll to have a look at the new Olympic Stadium which was in the process of being completed, then also visiting the apartments which we knew we would be using for the Games the following year. Of course, as it turned out we didn't know anything of the sort and a few months after that tournament, the world changed.

Broadcasting was transformed, along with everything else, and so much that has been altered might take a while to return to the way it was – if it ever does. And, as you would have learned from reading these pages, a large part of the change involves not travelling to certain events, but commentating instead from studios in the UK.

This does have some advantages. Broadcasters – or their voices at least – are able to travel around the world at little expense and it does have other benefits in terms of flexibility and logistics. I recently had an offer to fill in as commentator on the Lions rugby tour of South Africa, which is another sporting event that is being covered remotely. It was very nearly possible but unfortunately to travel from Japan (Salford) to South Africa (West London) in two and a half hours would have been cutting it very fine indeed and not even bringing with it the bonus of air miles. Besides, those who were keen followers of both athletics and rugby, switching from one channel to another, may also have seen through the artifice of it all.

As it happens, a lot of people do believe we are out there in Japan just now and while you never lie and explicitly say that you are, by mentioning the weather or the atmosphere 'here in the stadium', or talking of the light supper you had with the Emperor last night, you try not to disabuse the viewers of that notion either. So, any number of messages come in telling me that I must be missing my dogs or that I will get quite a welcome when I return home. As it happens those correspondents are correct on both fronts, but I know that I am currently missing them for just a few hours at a time and yes, their welcome will be quite something – but only because it is the same overload of excitement whether I return from Greater Manchester or six thousand miles further east.

Of course, television has long since been a world of some illusion, but we do seem to be living in an increasingly artificial world. While we do have reporters out in Japan, all presentation and commentary is being done from back here. We spend our days (nights) in a giant recording studio which is more often the venue for BBC orchestra performances or recordings of radio plays. Now, a series of cubicles have been constructed for coverage of the various sports which are often taking place at the same time and we all shout away as if in a giant commentary farm, or a particularly animated call centre.

The presenters, meanwhile, sit in a studio which is entirely green, using the green-screen technology that allows an image to be digitally created around them. It's more properly called 'chroma key' and you see it every day in films or news reports, or perhaps most commonly in weather forecasts where the presenter appears to be standing in front of a map, but all they have behind them is a green or blue screen. They are helped out by having monitors and a faint outline projected onto the screen, so that they do get some assistance to prevent them talking about the rainfall approaching East Anglia while simultaneously waving their hands over the Outer Hebrides. In fact, any colour could be isolated to use for the screen but they are most commonly green or blue because they are the colours on the spectrum which differ most from human skin tone.

For the Olympics coverage this means that the audience at home sees a couple of beautifully created studios

– in the morning a Japanese garden, in the evening a dramatic penthouse looking out over the Tokyo skyline – but in reality, all is green. The strict instruction therefore is that neither presenter nor guests can wear anything of that colour since whatever they had chosen would become part of a plant or a building or a neon sign and if they decided to go for an entire *ensemble vert* they would appear only as a floating head talking about the tae kwon do.

And, perhaps appropriately, being green may dictate more of this kind of thing in the future. Now, and for a long time beyond this pandemic, there are environmental issues to consider – issues that become more obviously pressing with every river that floods or tree that burns. The days of sizeable production teams taking flights to locations may be over, when the job can be done from back home. It would not be of precisely the same quality – commentary is always a fraction better when fully immersed in the event, surrounded by the noise and the colour ourselves, but as the incoming messages confirm, it is not always noticeable to the viewer. Besides, I am sure that we will all have plenty of sacrifices to make in the years ahead – different attitudes to travel for work or for play.

Tonight, as it turns out, even my remote work is cancelled. I am supposed to be commentating on the rugby sevens from Tokyo, but my co-commentator has been 'pinged', to use a word which is entirely of the moment

– snagged by proximity to a positive case, or perhaps just wandering too close to somebody else's phone. It is another aspect of modern broadcasting and work in general which is changing the way we have to operate.

So instead I watch from my own sofa in the early hours, with both dogs alongside me as deeply unqualified co-commentators, who offer little insight when Fiji win the men's title as they did in Rio. Like their fellow players from the ill-fated autumn tournament, members of the Fijian squad haven't been able to return to their closed-off island home for the past fourteen months. Exiles from their own land, tears come easily as they sing and celebrate this rare gold medal for their country. There is nothing at all artificial about their overwhelming joy.

Friday 30 July

Another day of being awake in the dark and sleeping in the light – living in a negative. Heading into work at about 10 p.m., there is, I confess, something I quite like about it. Going against the conventional flow of human life and moving around when all is quiet. The only difficulty is in then sitting in a darkened room at three in the morning and staring at a hot, bright and humid Tokyo, trying to be as animated and energetic as if you were there. But my metamorphosis into a creature of the night is complete. It turns out that I am now the mole, industriously tunnelling away as people sleep. And the mounds of earth which I leave for them to find are the recorded highlights of the qualifying rounds in the 800 metres, shown on the breakfast round-up programme.

There is a break between sessions in the athletics in Tokyo, which does offer a chance to grab an hour or two of rest in the early morning here, but then we have to get up again at 8 a.m. to start preparing for commentary once more, which will carry on through until about two in the afternoon. This shift-pattern would be considered cruel to actual moles – prodded awake and forced to get up and clock on again in the morning and then so confused that they would start to dig in the wrong direction, or fall asleep mid-worm.

My method for counteracting these ill-effects is to drink as much coffee as is humanly possible, which does work very effectively for a short while, but a comprehensive crash always occurs during the session. This happens some time mid-morning in the UK where my body is to be found, mid-evening in Tokyo which is where my mind currently resides. Meanwhile my sleep patterns are lost somewhere over Siberia on a flight which I never took.

In fact, it appears that I have successfully managed to create jet lag without going anywhere. And since it is now the only part of air travel that I have had the chance to experience of late, I wonder if I should go all out and recreate every other aspect. Perhaps wandering about with a sleep pillow wrapped around my neck and buying a carton of two hundred cigarettes and some cut-price Ray-Bans. Then curling up in a small chair and having people bump me every five minutes or so on their way to the bathroom.

As it is, I doze for a couple of hours in the afternoon and, if I have the energy, I make the drive home to do so. While more appealing than a hotel, this does, however, come with its own issues of potential disturbance and after today's incident I will make sure that the door to the bedroom is firmly shut lest a small, blonde intruder should wonder where I am, creep up the stairs to investigate and awaken me from precious sleep by waving a damp stuffed owl in my face.

Yet I could never get angry with Mabel as she is just so delighted to see me back again from Japan and still so very, very pleased with her owl. Although I do spare a thought for another nocturnal creature which is going through its own gruelling routine.

AUGUST 2021

Saturday 7 August

After a certain amount of time covering an event like the Olympics, you find that you exist for that purpose and that alone. You have the time and energy to perform only the essential tasks, into which category projects such as keeping a record of life and musing upon it, do not fall – hence the extended diary absence. Instead, you withdraw to maintaining the function of only two vital organs: 1) the work that is asked of you and 2) sleeping, while everything else in your life is forgotten or slips into disrepair – including my diet, which is now approximately ninety per cent cake and pastry-based.

Yet before I reached this stage – and perhaps because it is somehow still deemed a vital function – I did manage to find time to put out an Olive and Mabel Olympics video a few days ago and it seems to have gone down well. Once more it was trying to reflect current goings-on in our own world, but clearly Mabel's efforts in the fox-shit rolling event have also managed to strike a chord with fellow dog owners.

Of course, it is helped in its humour by having a bit of the comedy of the absurd, but – and it might only be because I am close to hallucinating at this point – I now start to look at our own human sporting events and wonder if they are really any more sensible. Indeed, so many sports can seem odd when you take pause to consider them. Not necessarily athletics, for what could be more simple and obvious than running faster, throwing further or jumping higher than somebody else? Yet there are any number of sports which bear all the hallmarks of having been thought up during a late-night drinking session – with everybody prepared to go along with it the next morning because their heads hurt too much to protest. Golf or ice hockey or snooker or water polo and a hundred more which you would think would fail to pass the initial planning stage, before I even start on the intricacies and complexities of cricket or rugby union to which any dissenting voice might reasonably say, 'Look, perhaps we should develop the one where our pets roll in excrement instead.'

So why do we create them all? What is the point and the purpose of sport?

For one man, it was the idea that physical effort and competition would lead to all manner of social benefits – Baron Pierre de Coubertin, who was the main driving force behind the foundation of the modern Olympic Games. A Parisian aristocrat and educator, de Coubertin was greatly taken with the moral and physical teachings offered at English public schools – in particular after spending some time at Rugby School, famous as the birthplace of the sport of rugby football and also as the setting for the fictional work *Tom Brown's School Days*.

Surrounded by such robust health and muscular achievement, de Coubertin saw what he felt were the enormously positive effects of physical education, observing that 'organised sport can create moral and social strength', preventing minds from becoming idle whereby they would doubtless discover less organised things to do instead, things which might be equally enjoyable, but not perhaps morally upstanding – or indeed activities that you should win awards for at the annual school sports day. By contrast, a healthy body would lead to a healthy mind and great success would follow as it had for Britain during its rise to global dominance in the nineteenth century, a prosperity which was, according to de Coubertin, built on the culture and competition of the playing fields of the public schools. He tried to replicate this model in the French education system without much success, so instead turned his attention to his other great passion – a revival of the ancient Games of Olympia.

It wasn't that he was an outstanding sportsman himself. He did actually win an Olympic gold medal, although this was awarded for literature at the 1912 Games in Stockholm where they held competitions in the arts as well – which sounds very much as if they were including them purely in order to let the boss win something. We are told that he entered his poem 'Ode to Sport' under a pseudonym, although there is always the possibility that he dropped it on the desk of the judges and said, 'WELL now, here's a good one I fancy,' whilst winking.

But, his own lack of sporting prowess aside, de Coubertin more importantly saw what he believed sport could do for others. Apart from anything else he felt that sport would build *character* and that organised competition would better us all. That having a race would improve the human race.

Yet sport all too often now seems to bring out our darker side.

Yesterday, in the very small window between finishing my work for the day and welding my face to a pillow for three vital hours, I watched some of the modern pentathlon, a sport which de Coubertin himself invented. It is based upon the idea of an officer behind enemy lines trying to evade capture – hence the five disciplines of shooting, swimming, fencing, horse-riding and running.

It is unlikely that the leader in the women's event would agree with the notion of sport building character, as her own seemed to be dissolving in front of us. In modern pentathlon, you draw lots to see which horse you will mount for the showjumping element – again replicating the notion that you have just come upon this unfamiliar creature in a field. And that is clearly where this horse wanted to be, as it refused to do anything that was asked of it, at which point the officer behind enemy lines would be penning a letter to loved ones and breaking open the vial of cyanide. Here, the face of the soon-to-be ex-leader crumpled in desperate tears at seeing her open-top bus parade through Berlin disappear at the whim of a recalcitrant animal.

I suppose this was at least sport as entertainment since we watched with a morbid fascination as the horse either put the brakes on at a fence or stood looking thoroughly pissed off that it had been asked to do this on its Friday night. It all reminded me greatly of the Beijing Games in 2008 when I had been required to commentate on the modern pentathlon. There, one of the leaders in the men's event came unstuck in similar fashion with a horse which, when shown a fence to jump said, 'Now why in God's name would I want to do that?' then went and parked itself in the corner while the rider convulsed in the saddle as the seconds ticked away and I, without much of a clue as to what was happening, could only utter general commentary along the lines of 'Ooooh. Now...that's unfortunate.'

It simply highlights the oddness of what we call sport and brings further questions as to why we do it. Of course, it is an entertaining diversion – we all know the essential fun of sporting activities. After all, animals love play as well – dogs with sticks or balls, cats with bits of string, killer whales with semi-conscious, very depressed seals. But, as with many things, we have taken the simple animal concept – the essence – and added so many layers. We humans aren't satisfied with merely having the fun of doing the activity. We need to show that we can do it brilliantly. We need to win, or at the very least compete. Perhaps it comes back to a search for glory and that desire for recognition or approval that we see in so many other walks of life. Which means that our overinflated version of sport can take us to euphoric highs or leave us in a very troubled state – perhaps even crying hysterically on a horse.

It now emerges this evening that one of the coaches of the German modern pentathlon team has been sent home from Japan after punching the unhelpful animal and I wonder if this is what de Coubertin had in mind when he grew misty-eyed with love for sport and what the Olympic Games might do for humanity all those years ago.

So what lessons do we learn here? We are so often told that sport is not about the winning, it's about the taking part – it was a fundamental belief of de Coubertin himself: 'L'important c'est de participer.' Yet sometimes for humans it is clearly only about the winning.

And for animals, it is sometimes about not being at all interested in doing either of those things.

Sunday 8 August

In for the final day of coverage from Salford-upon-Tokyo. Although I really exist in no specific place now and merely float in non-corporeal form – a voice saying stuff about sport from somewhere.

Not an end-of-term feeling of relaxation though, as the closing ceremony is almost as demanding as the opening was sixteen days ago, but it also requires a certain reflection. It asks for well-structured thoughts and a wise judgement to be passed on individuals and the Games as a whole, when your brain is only capable of vague noises lasting no more than one syllable. Thus, upon seeing athlete upon athlete pile into the stadium, the considered opinion which is offered is more likely to be, 'Ah…nice…they good…win gold.'

Yet, after a small vat of coffee I am able to expand a little more and observe that if one thing has stood out at this Olympic Games, it has been the sport taking place with far more emotion attached to it amidst a near-constant exposure of the feelings of those who compete.

In putting together a montage of great moments at the end of a Games, we might, in the past, have suggested the shot of the athlete who cried on the podium or during an interview, to which a producer this year would ask us to narrow it down to our favourite five or six. Indeed, somebody who doesn't over-emote in an interview is now abnormal. If the athlete in question merely says, 'Yes, not too bad. Could have been better I suppose…' we will hurl things at the TV, shouting, 'What are you, some kind of ROBOT?' or just sigh and change channels, because we now demand emotion to go with the sporting achievement. We have added another layer.

And yet there are plenty of sportspeople who are able to emote for us, because sport during a pandemic is pressure and the willing admittance of it. Athletes and competitors are the same as all of us – on edge. There is a release of sentiment which they might not have known they were storing up, but which comes flooding out in anger and frustration or joy and relief. All they have gone through and given up to be here – to train under lock-down, to see that their lifelong dream of the Olympics might or might not happen, then to make the trip after everything and it goes horribly wrong or wonderfully right. Well, all the interviewer has to do then is remind them of that – plus mention anything to do with family, friends or beloved cockapoo Sugar Puff watching back home and the lip will tremble and eyes start to glisten.

So we talk of compassion and understanding – we are now far more aware of mental health issues in the world at large. Yet competitive sport can be viewed differently. It's probably not designed for a more sensitive world of trying to make sure that nobody has their feelings hurt and resolve tested or nerve exposed, because that is exactly what competition will do. By its very nature, it is going to reward some people and upset others.

Yet despite all of that, the other thing it is capable of is bringing so many people together – which is clearly on display at the closing ceremony. Initially, as all the countries come into the stadium they are firmly within their own groups – the gangs of friends arriving at the school dance and remaining tethered to their own cliques. But as it moves on, the mingling increases and by the end you realise that the hoary speeches extolling unity and togetherness are perhaps not so far from the truth and de Coubertin was onto something after all. Although that might just be me looking at it in my own tired and over-emotional state.

And from my point of view, it has just been a very different Games. I would dearly loved to have been out in Tokyo – covering this Olympics has been a pale imitation of past events, as many people have found their work in recent times. But you have to look at the positives of it and the advantage has been some more time with Olive and Mabel.

I know that I have had more than my fair share of them in recent months but, when eventually they have gone to lie on the eternal sofa, what would I do for two more weeks of their company? To have them clattering across the floor, bodies shaking with joy at my return. To sit in the garden with them on either side, chewing at grass or staring at a flower or perhaps a passing butterfly. To lower my head into their soft heads and sleeping forms and tell them quietly that I love them. Well, for that I would gladly trade every trip I have ever made and every great event I have seen.

Tuesday 10 August

Olive and Mabel can be so annoying.

This is mostly down to their point-blank refusal to come when called or to stop eating grass when requested to do so. In particular their walk up the lane is proving almost impossible, with lush green verges on either side – to them this lane is now akin to a walk through a tunnel lined with cheese and sausages. Today there is the added temptation of a particular brand of horse manure which seems to meet with their approval. Both make frequent stops to chew away at the soft, brown piles lying in the dust and when I shout at them, look slightly bemused as if I am missing out – in their eyes I am simply a fussy eater.

Further on, Olive has paused for one of her many more verdant grazing sessions, my increasingly frustrated calls to get her to move as unsuccessful as the rider in the modern pentathlon – met only with a defiant stare and a smack of her chops as the blades gradually disappear like a string of spaghetti sucked in by a child. Mabel ignores me entirely – not because she is being wilfully resistant, but because she can only focus on one thing at a time. And at the moment that thing is grass, which she licks and nibbles far less effectively than her half-dog, half-cow friend.

At this point a car comes down the lane and stops beside us with the driver, who I recognise as a fan of Olive and Mabel, winding down the window to have a word.

'This is all your fault you know…' she says, and when seeing my questioning expression, points to the back seat. 'THIS…'

There, in a crate, rising up to chew at my fingers through the top bars with the sharpest of puppy teeth, is a tiny black Labrador. I'm told that this is Ethel, and Ethel is as enthusiastic about life as it is possible to be. Just starting a journey of a dozen years or more where that enthusiasm, kindliness and joy will barely diminish and will be passed on to everybody she meets.

It's not the first time that I have been told by new dog owners that they were inspired to get a dog based upon the Olive and Mabel appearances last year – or at the very least, it was the final confirmation that they should make the move. I hope people understand what they are getting into and that, if they are getting dogs after watching Olive and Mabel, that they are not going to feel enormously disappointed when their own dogs do not help build furniture, take an active part in poker sessions or are capable of having their annual appraisals via Zoom.

But then again, it is the more mundane normality of dogs which is their great strength at the moment in this unsettled, abnormal world.

Today, people continue to express themselves in a summer of discontent as anti-vaxxers storm the BBC, with their intention to invade the newsroom and disrupt what they see as the spread of misinformation. They arrive en masse at Television Centre in West London and film themselves trying to force their way in through the main door – not initially dissuaded upon being told that the BBC isn't here anymore, having sold up and moved out eight years ago. Possibly they believe it is all part of the lie. Only after a lengthy episode of pushing, shouting and recording their mission statements while wearing military-style berets, do they grudgingly accept that the building to which they are laying siege really is now a combination of residential apartments and a couple of studios for hire where, among other things, the chat show *Loose Women* is recorded. And that isn't being filmed today.

So they head off to Central London, promising to attack the actual BBC newsroom once they work out exactly where it is. And still so very, very angry about it all. They really could have benefitted from meeting Ethel.

Sunday 15 August

'No man is an island, entire of itself; every man is a piece of the continent, a part of the main...

...Any man's death diminishes me, because I am involved in mankind, and therefore never send to know for whom the bell tolls; it tolls for thee.'

Meditation Number 17 (JOHN DONNE, 1623)

I could write something light-hearted about dogs tonight. Perhaps about how Olive threw up a decent amount of grass in the sitting room and blithely pretended that nothing had happened, or that Mabel got so excited about an impending ball-throwing session that she ran into a wall. But sometimes I am aware that life is also about people.

In fact, all the time you are aware of it. It's just that you involve yourself in frivolous matters to help you escape – so that you don't hear each and every human misdeed and misfortune for fear of going mad. But then it shouts so loudly to make you turn your head.

The already blighted country of Haiti has been devastated this weekend by another earthquake and today comes a story of misery which is entirely man-made, as the former structure in Afghanistan is swept away. The capacity that humans have – or a few at least – to inflict distress and suffering on others is seemingly endless.

It leaves people in a wretched situation. People for whom the desire to travel and be somewhere else and leading a different life is now urgent and real and not a petty frustration or some whimsical idea brought on by a sort of ennui. We know that we are all connected but still retreat to, and live in, our very separate and starkly different worlds. We also know that we must pay attention and we must do something, because to not see or not care would make you self-absorbed or a sociopath – and it is really best to be neither of those things.

Yet sometimes we don't quite know what to do or how to help, so we only stress again to each other that we really must do something, while returning to whatever is occupying us here – grateful for the trivial concerns that come with fortunate lives.

Monday 16 August

Waken at 3.30 this morning. By choice. Although still not entirely willingly. And also very slowly.

After the alarm clock had performed its solemn duty, I had that momentary lack of knowledge of who I was, where I was, or what I might be doing here and this was followed by a few clouded seconds of Kafka-esque assessment of the situation as the cogs of my brain ground into life. Finally I remembered that I was in a hotel at the start of a very long day indeed, in which we would play one hole on eighteen different golf courses up the east coast of Scotland, all the way from North Berwick in East Lothian to Cruden Bay, about twenty-five miles north of Aberdeen.

I say we, because I was accompanied in this frivolous endeavour by a man possessing actual golfing talent – tour player Andrew 'Beef' Johnston, as well as a sizeable film crew which would capture each moment and every angle of the day on behalf of the European Tour. Sadly, neither Olive nor Mabel had been allowed to come along on this one – much to their annoyance when they heard that I was travelling with Beef and imagined that he might be an enormous golfing sirloin.

It's best to draw a veil over the sporting performance of one half of the partnership and indeed much of the day itself, as the accumulated sleep deprivation of the past couple of months caught up with me and I wallowed in a low humour. Yet it is certainly worth recounting that I met a good few dogs along the way who I will always gravitate towards as morale-boosters. An early one came shortly after 5.30 a.m. and still long before breakfast, as we arrived at our second golf course and met the greenkeepers who were preparing for their day's graft. Accompanying them in their work was a giant and gentle-looking soul who was called Oscar – equal parts dog, horse and bear, he was shackled by a lead to one of the greenkeeper's vehicles.

'Could I untie him to say hello properly?' I ask one of them.

'I'm not sure, he's a wee bit lively...'

At which point most people would take the hint, accept the warning for the good sense that it is, perhaps administer a final scratch of the ear and thereafter move on, wishing everyone a most pleasant day. Yet for some reason I have never properly listened to advice – as if I believe that the person offering it might be misguided or perhaps doesn't even really mean it. I also, for reasons that are entirely unclear, consider myself some sort of dog whisperer who can control even the most unhinged animal with a soothing word or just by staring into its eyes and humming gently, like Crocodile Dundee.

So here I smile, in beatific fashion, reassuring all with my great dog wisdom and, laying a magical hand upon his head, unclip the dog-horse-bear, saying, 'Don't worry, I think I know how to han…' which is a sentence never to be completed as there is now only a slowly dissipating dog-shaped cloud where Oscar had once been. Oscar himself is already fifty yards away performing a few high-speed laps of the once perfectly manicured green.

'Here…come HERE…OSCAR…COME to me, dog…' I cry, holding up my three-iron as if, despite this very obvious setback, I have now promoted myself to the status of dog-commanding wizard. Eventually, after much chasing – a game which the giant Oscar had been enjoying immensely – the team of greenkeepers corrals him, one sneaking up unnoticed from the side to grab his collar and he is soon under lock and key again.

'Aye, that's why it's best to keep him tied up,' says the dog-keeper-in-chief and we make a hasty exit to the next course – Oscar panting heavily, but without too much emotion, through his post-match interview, the greenkeepers now busying themselves with a few more spike marks to work on and me just a little less sure of my truly amazing ability to commune with the animals.

As we drive past Edinburgh and out of Lothian, we travel over the wide Firth of Forth by the Queensferry

Crossing, enabling me to come up with all manner of witticisms about the first, second and third Forth bridges into Fife. And a short while after, Beef requesting that I don't make this day feel any longer than it already is.

Our journey is comfortable enough though – being made in an all-electric car as the film is partly to showcase the abilities of said vehicle. And it does seem very impressive, as well as offering a glimpse of a near-future which, you would imagine, is more certain than a multimillion-pound artwork floating in the digital ether. So, in exhaust-free fashion, we make our way round the coast of Fife and pass through villages and towns which at this time of year combine roles of working harbours and holiday destinations – all with an obvious charm and appeal as white cottages and solid, dark stone houses are lifted and coloured by the warm August sun.

Reaching Anstruther, a small harbour and town where the Forth blends into the North Sea, there is a stop for a crew change and lunch and we eat leaning on a sea wall, looking out at a large and glistening superyacht that sits rather conspicuously in waters more often frequented by tiny, weathered fishing boats. The glamorous vessel is at least given some help to blend in today by the blue sky, and the North Sea – so often grey and bitterly cold – has been offered a chance to dress up and sparkle like the Mediterranean on the Amalfi Coast.

'That's Tom Cruise out there…' says one of the locals with a nod to the visiting craft, although when pressed is unable to confirm any actual glimpses of the star. But social media is apparently awash with Cruise sightings and we are reliably informed that the very same boat – along with the man himself – was photographed in the seas off Cornwall. Apparently it is because he is here in the UK during production of the latest film in the *Mission Impossible* franchise and the work, as far as I can make out, so far seems to involve reccies for possible shooting locations at Wimbledon, the European Championship final at Wembley, several restaurants and a massive luxury yacht.

As we continue with our lower budget golfing road-trip movie here at Anstruther, the crowd which gathers to watch us play is entirely down to the appeal of Beef rather than internet rumours that two Labradors are in town making a film. While we are completing our designated hole (for golf geeks, the fifth at Anstruther, which is possibly the world's most difficult par-three), a few hundred yards out at sea the Good Ship Hollywood fires up its motors and starts to move. Perhaps they believe that the multitude is here for them, fixing long lenses on the boat and hoping for a glimpse of superstar torso – when the truth is they're watching me make a complete bollocks of a very simple shot from just off the green. But soon we are all on our way – Tom off to cruise elsewhere or perhaps even go and do some work. And us in our electric car, about which Beef suddenly has a question.

'Why's it making a noise like a car?'

It's a far more sensible enquiry than it first appears. If the car is electric – then why is it making the noise of a petrol-driven supercar when you touch the accelerator? Investigations soon reveal the answer, that it is currently on the setting to produce that kind of artificial engine noise and that, furthermore, there is a menu of options for pretend sounds of varying levels of ferocity. So, there we are – even when we have the silence, we can choose to add an unnecessary and unnatural layer. And for the last hundred miles we have been revving around like riders of a Harley Davidson who, in my experience, quite often need to be told the stark truth that they are not an easy rider or rebel without a cause but are actually a financial adviser in their mid-fifties.

Unsurprisingly, from this point on, I choose the silence. And in stealth mode, scattering tourists who step out in front of us fancying they hear nothing but the rustling of the wind, we pass through small towns with long beaches and venerable golf courses and I greet several more dogs, either straining to make it to their beach playground or returning with their fur matted by a special blend of salt water and sand. But all willing to chat for a moment and without fail accompanied by an owner who asks why Olive and Mabel aren't with me. We tick off St Andrews, of course, where I give a nod in the passing to the student days here of my very good friend Kate Middleton, then cross the Tay and, with the sun seeming to lower at an alarming rate, we fire off rapid golf shots at Arbroath and Montrose, Royal Aberdeen and Murcar.

Finally we reach our last course at Cruden Bay and by now the race is lost – all is pitch black. And it is largely my fault, caused by regular dog chats, as well as frequent loss of balls and temper and – for one very long half-hour – a mislaid car key. So, when we walk out to the hole which we are going to take on, we only know that we are playing on massive dunes high above the breaking sea as we can hear it somewhere off in the void below and we duly complete this epic round of golf just after 11 p.m. – under the lights of the greenkeepers' trucks and maintenance vehicles which, even at full beam, struggle to push too far out into the darkness.

I'm sad to report there was no friendly canine turf assistant tied up here to bookend the day. Although I did notice a pair of bright and wary eyes that were caught briefly by the torches and headlamps, then disappeared as the creature turned away and stalked off into the longer grass. It might have been a cat or a fox or a deer – I couldn't really tell and what's more had lost all confidence in trying to summon it with my magical animal powers. But before I fall into welcome sleep tonight, I will make sure to go on the internet and announce it as another confirmed sighting of Tom Cruise.

Thursday 19 August

It is very interesting to see how different people have taken to the readjustment of life – the re-instatement of the norm, with plenty keen to carry on as before but reverting in an immediate transformation, as if they have snapped themselves out of a nightmare and as they lie with relief upon sweated sheets, they now consider it over and done.

My resurfacing will be a slower, steadier climb. Continuing to wear a mask indoors is something which I am still reluctant to abandon, although today as I walk around an enormous shopping centre – and with every day that passes – there does seem to be a shifting in the balance and it might not be too long before people are pointing and laughing at the funny man. I'm not sure where this cautious attitude comes from as it is so very far from my approach to any other aspect of life. But it just seems like the sensible thing to do and it's not hurting anybody else – which, you might add, is exactly the aim.

One of the major drawbacks of the mask, though, is the concealment of facial expressions. Human beings have evolved over thousands of years to detect and inter-pret the very small changes in a face. Quite apart from those who need to read lips, almost everybody, whether you know it or not, is able to judge in a fraction what-ever emotion or intent another person is harbouring. We see immediately if they are kind, friendly, amusing or hostile and respond accordingly with warmth, aggression or bribery.

My problem is that my face does have a tendency to rest in a scowl and occasionally I might not even mean it. So, where possible, I have sometimes given what I hope is a rather kindly smile, to let people know that I really do mean no harm to them or their friends and family. In reality it is no more than a feeble upturn of the corners of my mouth, but it can make a big difference to my otherwise angry face – although perhaps in reality just adds a hint of psychosis. Yet with that pleasantly smiling cum vaguely unhinged option no longer available, I am requiring everything above the mask to take on the extra workload and so I now raise my eyebrows extravagantly in an attempt to indicate goodwill. Although I realise now that it could be interpreted as if everything is taking me by surprise. Which it often is.

The major event of the day – and yes, it is a quiet time – comes this evening as, upon opening the back door to release the dogs for their last outing of the day, a cat is seen sitting just a few yards away, heavily involved in the process of cleaning itself. All parties are momentarily stunned, with my eyebrows, for once, raised in genuine curiosity. It must be one of the cats belonging to a neighbouring farm – a hardened feline of the outdoors who has no doubt seen some sights and handled bigger threats than two dogs who come from a life of soft furnishings and chamomile-infused biscuits before bedtime.

Olive and Mabel initially seem unsure as to what to do since neither of them has seen a cat for some time and I think had hoped that they had become extinct. But the memories all come flooding back and both sides quickly fall into long-established and familiar roles – Mabel making the first move, and within one or two nano-seconds at most, achieving the speed of sound. She is then subject to an even greater G-force in applying the brakes as the cat abandons its evasive run and instead decides to turn and hiss and swipe with its claws at the part of the air where it hopes Mabel's face will soon join them. Mabel's reaction – after a moment's regret that she couldn't read the facial signals of the cat – is to insist that she is 'not looking for any trouble' and then scamper back to the sanctuary of elder dog and human, having reached the conclusion that the outside world is sometimes not what you expect or want it to be.

Tuesday 24 August

I might as well apply for full citizenship of Salford. It now turns out that it is impossible to get a work visa for the United States in time to travel to the Ryder Cup next month. It's frustrating, in particular when it seems far more straightforward to travel in the opposite direction and I am contemplating marriage to a mail-order bride from Arkansas as a last resort. As long as she accepts that I will only return to help around the house when a major sporting event is taking place in the country.

We had in fact been told that we could expedite the visa process by explaining our situation, with special allowances made for those who are in dire need of travel for reasons such as attending a funeral or visiting an ill relative. But – in what I felt was a fairly brief email of reply – it was made abundantly clear to me that travelling there to describe golf balls being hit does not meet the necessary criteria. I then tried other avenues of persuasion as I couldn't help but notice that the head man over there is now a dog lover, even though one of his own has been banished from the White House after repeatedly biting people, horribly corrupted by power. So, in one more message I did disclose that I was a pretty big deal in the world of dog videos and I'm hoping that will be sufficient to change their minds and allow me in. Although I haven't heard back for some weeks now.

As a result – and because our presenter and various members of production staff are in the same non-visa-possessing situation, it is likely that we will be broadcasting from afar once more – in work or play, travel is not necessarily becoming any easier. America is off-limits, Japan remains on high alert as the Paralympics takes place, New Zealand is still determined to work its way through everything by snap lockdowns and a zero-tolerance approach towards the illness, while Australia has become a mythical land, like Atlantis. We are told it once existed, somewhere, but now wonder if it ever did beyond our imaginations.

So we will continue to wait and hope that things improve – as they surely must. And in the meantime, I will have to be content with a forthcoming trip to Bury St Edmunds.

Thursday 26 August

Warm and sunny again. It has been for a while and with the holidays in full swing and plenty who don't want to partake of the regulations involved to travel abroad, almost the entire population has now taken up residency in Cornwall, to the extent that the country might topple bow over stern and sink beneath the waters of the North Atlantic, with Kate Winslet and Leonardo DiCaprio clinging on for dear life at John O'Groats. Fortunately there are just about enough people who have made their way to the Lake District or the Highlands to counterbalance it and we remain stable. But almost everybody has headed for the open spaces of the beaches or the hills and if not there, then they are roaming the countryside in campervans and adopting the ancient and traditional ways of the British nomad, sitting on folding chairs in a layby with a cup of tea and listening to the Archers.

These really are the dog days. Olive and Mabel lounge around and we slow down as well, as emails only trigger a thousand out of office replies – automatic notices that have been stating the obvious for quite a while now. But this is the time of year where business ticks along more quietly and approaches bearing news of interesting projects certainly fall away – when you start to wonder if you should have accepted that offer to do commentary on a Saturday evening gameshow or film yourself reading a newspaper for an Instagram post.

There is still news to entertain us though and I see that one schoolboy is bucking the trend by doing brisk business in the holidays, creating and selling another example of NFT art. I think it worth clarifying here that I'm not becoming obsessed with NFTs, it's just that they seem to say a great deal about the madness of our modern world. And, unfortunately, the more I investigate them, the more the internet decides that I must be very interested in becoming an early adopter – thus greatly increasing their visibility as I am served up a regular diet of NFT-based stories mixed in with ads for dog dressing-gowns.

I would also like to think that as I experience more of the NFT business, I would begin to further understand it, but in fact I am heading in the opposite direction. In this example, it seems that instead of playing on a beach, riding a bike or climbing a tree over the summer, the twelve-year-old in question has created a series of thousands of tiny graphics of whales. Which is great – everybody has to have a hobby. Yet this is now far more than an idle pastime as somebody who is spending their summer in equally unconventional fashion has bought it for $290,000. This is transferred in the form of Ethereum, a cryptocurrency which he could cash in or wait to see if it rises or falls in value, which seems to be tied to confidence, or lack of it, in the whole idea. And since cryptocurrency seems to do either of those things in regular and dramatic fashion, if I were advising the youngster I would say to him, take the $290,000 for the cartoon whales. But I do think again how strange it is and a decidedly odd way to spend one's time and energies.

This evening I spend two or three hours selecting the final twelve Labradors for a charity calendar. You would think it should be a fairly straightforward task, but I take it all a bit too seriously and deliberate at great length over every decision. 'Nice ears in this one, but I don't know if I'm really *feeling* November when I look at it?' Some of the photos are action shots, others are sleeping and there are plenty where the dog sits uncomfortably having obviously been manoeuvred into position, told to sit a while and is now concentrating so very hard on doing the right thing to please the human behind the camera. But you know that, to each owner, their beloved dog is the most appealing in the world, so there is a reluctance to reject any of them. It is surely similar to that blindness of parentage, whereby every newborn baby is a thing of exceptional beauty – except to my mother, who will insist on telling anybody who might care to listen that one of my brothers was quite hideous for the first six months or so.

Eventually I whittle it down to the required dozen

and I have to console myself with the thought that those who are not chosen will still be absolutely sure that their dog is the most beautiful dog of all. And I am very pleased indeed that this calendar will be put up on a household wall or two around the country – some people have a year to come which will be presented to them entirely through the medium of dogs. Labradors always watching them – dominating every day of their lives. As if you can possibly imagine such a thing.

SEPTEMBER 2021

Thursday 2 September

I pass some time this afternoon by trying to film a sort of trailer for our forthcoming theatre tour, which begins on Sunday.

I say filming, as if it might be a major production, whereas it is of course just me with my phone. And I say a trailer, but really it's only an attempt to get either dog to take – and then for the grand finale, leave – a ball.

Yet neither dog seems to have the requisite dedication to the task and, in tandem with my growing frustration at Olive's determination to hold onto the ball which she has been given, they soon grow bored and drift off to do their own things. Naturally, as I stop filming, Olive begins to roll on her back with a performance of gymnastic artistry that would audition strongly for Cirque du Soleil, although as I press record again she senses that she is now being watched and begins to wrap it up, just to annoy me. But then I notice, at the edge of frame, that Mabel has also halted whatever pointless activity she was doing and is now on full alert, vibrating nervously. The reason becomes clear when my ears attune, as hers evidently have, to the noise of a bee. It is incredibly high-pitched, as if the bee in question is dreadfully anguished about something – possibly the number of its friends and colleagues who have recently taken to wandering very slowly on the ground, mumbling 'carry on without me'. But whatever the reason, the bee falsetto has hit that wavelength which makes Mabel believe that we're all going to die in some hideous fashion.

So now, before me, is laid out the very obvious difference between these two dogs. Olive starts to roll again, scratching joyfully on the grass without a care in the world, while Mabel is traumatised by insect chat. She who has only barked about three or four times in her life – and greatly surprised herself on each one of those occasions – now stares into the bush shouting in her fear and angst, reversing away and then stepping forward again as boldly as she dare. Why, she wonders are we not all aware of the danger as she is? Why is Olive treating it so casually? It is a manifest example of everybody being wired to look at life in a different way. And she continues to growl into the plants and flowers, tentative exclamations emerging from puffed cheeks, quite certain that there is a tiny man in there with a tiny chainsaw come to do away with us all.

In this, I suppose, Mabel is simply reflecting the

feelings of many of us – trying to deal with more neuro-
ses than we used to, more anxious and concerned about
something…about everything. Although I'm not sure
what her excuse was before the pandemic since she has
been like this for four and a half years. The only means
of soothing her is to occupy her mind with another matter, knowing that it can only be tuned into one channel.
So I fetch the tennis balls and manage to switch her over
to a light entertainment programme as they both race
around, catching them at the third or fourth attempt,
crashing into bushes to take both object of desire and
a long snout full of leaves. Mabel has now entirely forgotten what was vexing her and skips gleefully back
towards me, to return the ball and receive her praise.

'You'd better get your shit together for Sunday night,'
I say to her, as she loudly hacks up two or three frothing
strands of clematis.

This evening, I decide to hold off on the release of
any dog garden footage, since the impending first date
of our tour is rather overshadowed in show-business
matters by one of the main news items of the day –
that ABBA are re-forming. It is a brief and entertaining
diversion from headlines of doom.

There is announcement of an album of new material
and, what's more, there will be a live tour. Although
'live' is a word here of some flexibility as there is a catch
– the performers seen on stage will be virtual representations of the Swedish foursome and furthermore they

will be based on their physical appearance from 1979. They seem quite specific about the year. Perhaps that is when the group decided they looked at their very finest and that Anni-Frida's earlier perm and Bjorn's platform boots had ruled out going back any further.

Accompanied by a genuinely live orchestra in the venue, the four avatars have been painstakingly and very cleverly modelled on the actual band members who will, in fact, be performing so that you do hear ABBA as they are now, it's just that those sounds will be coming from elsewhere and what you will see will be this artificial rendering. Therefore a young, vibrant Benny will be able to bounce at the piano, Agnetha can smile as she did to win a million hearts, all four will be smooth-skinned and youthful but elsewhere, perhaps sealed off in an attic, the more aged four will shuffle around as they really are.

Apparently it is being done this way because there is a reluctance from some members to be out there on the stage performing, facing a crowd. Facing other aspects of reality may also be a factor. Or maybe it is simply an acceptance that the fans would prefer it this way – to have their idols remain permanently as they once were, since for them to age reminds us that we have too. As has been noted before, nostalgia is often an overpowering yet comforting illusion. So now technology is only helping us to maintain it, knowing that we forever dance youthfully in our memories.

Sunday 5 September

Tonight the greasepaint was applied and we felt the building of nervous energy on hearing the eager anticipation from the stalls. Tonight we stood as performers again in that pool of bright light. Ah…sweet Madame Theatre, our old flame reignited – how we revelled in the sensations that came flooding back from our long and glorious career on the stage, in that one appearance in Cheltenham.

We are in Bury St Edmunds, for the first evening of our small tour of theatres around the country. It is the established way of course – take it to the provinces and try it out before the West End comes calling again. Although we won't hold our breath – an action which I'm almost certain that no dog has ever willingly performed anyway. Billed as *A Night with Olive and Mabel*, I had only hoped that it prove to be more exciting than an actual night with them lying on their backs and occasionally asking to go out into the garden, because I was again thinking of all those who had gone out of their way to buy a ticket and was so fearing the worst. *A Night with Olive and Mabel* was surely destined to be a flop – it is what Bialystock & Bloom had actually been looking for in *The Producers*.

I had therefore thought that it might be a good idea to make things more dramatic – put on a proper show, perhaps with a grand entrance by Olive and Mabel rising up through a trapdoor in the stage, appearing through a cloud of dry ice with 'Sirius' by the Alan Parsons Project filling the auditorium. Or all three of us could take the audience by surprise, bursting through the doors at the back and racing down the aisles, ears flapping and high-five-ing anybody within reach in a wanton breach of current sanitation protocols. Yet I quickly disregarded all such nonsensical plans for fear of alarming Mabel any more than was necessary and so, instead, we merely began with the lights dimming and the 'Canine Pour Chiens' perfume ad playing in the darkness – before host Emily Dean welcomed me on stage. I once again appeared initially alone, keeping the audience in suspense for only a few seconds, before the dog stars took their cue and galloped out from the wings, not in the least discomfited by the noise of the applause and the cheers, just running happily towards me wherever I might be.

And again, that moment must be the thrill for those who have come – to watch those dogs whom they already feel they know, stepping out of the videos. It certainly is the thrill of it for me to witness it in reverse, to see hundreds of faces belonging to those who have been behind other screens. It is the positive side of social media come to life as we all emerge in bodily form out of the ether.

As is customary, though, I did have further concerns. I wondered if people might be somewhat surprised to see them appear entirely as dogs...by which I mean that Olive and Mabel play characters in the videos and are presented in vaguely anthropomorphic form. So here, when I clip them onto leads and walk around with them it might be a shock, as if it is thoroughly degrading for these two major stars to be shackled in this way. Would I do this to the Two Ronnies at the height of their fame? Well, if Barker had no clue about traffic and Corbett a penchant for playing with cows in a field then yes, I most certainly would.

There is also the slight worry that they are being seen out of character – or at least people will see aspects of their personalities which I have either exaggerated by a small degree or kept entirely hidden. For example, I try not to let it be known that, on meeting people for the first time, Mabel does have reservations and can be a little uncertain, until slowly and steadily won over with constant physical affection. Therefore, confronted by six hundred people she might not initially seem quite the jolly, clownish figure of the screen and would actually appear rather introverted, like so many of the great comics.

Or perhaps somebody tonight will quite simply see through the whole thing and realise the emperor is naked. With Olive and Mabel not conversing with me and instead merely lying in their baskets an audience member will rise and with a voice that rings around the theatre, shout, 'Hang on everyone...don't you see? THEY'RE JUST A COUPLE OF DOGS!' Which, although entirely true, might break the spell. Whoever sees them through these eyes can never watch the videos in the same way again.

But thankfully it seems that everybody continues to suspend their disbelief or, more likely, doesn't care or analyse it quite as much as I do, and it's a very enjoyable evening. It takes on a decidedly interactive feel as well – the fourth wall crashing down in a strong piece of Brechtian Theatre as I lead them off stage and into the crowd. I try to demonstrate how truly useless they are as retrievers by placing the stuffed, squeaky rabbit and the ever-startled owl in the aisles, holding the dogs with a mighty command and then asking them to fetch. Of course, neither of them waits, distracted by illicit treats and dozens of wandering, affectionate hands and my standing as a dog master lies in tatters on the ground, alongside their equally dismantled reputation as dependable retrievers.

Later on, there is also a brief and entertaining appearance from Emily's Shih Tzu, Raymond, who had been left in her dressing room and has clearly been drinking heavily to pass the time. He pads around, making game attempts to join in with the other two – deciding that Olive, in particular, is looking rather fetching this evening, so rears up majestically on to his hind legs to look adoringly into her eyes, yet in the end has to settle for her knees. I'm not generally won over by dogs of a more compact size, but Raymond puts on quite a display – even if the overall effect is like a scene from *Beauty and the Beast* where a spell has brought a duster or a small mop to life for a song and dance routine with a candlestick. There's no doubt that Mabel is deeply uncertain as to what this new arrival actually is and backs away into the heavy black curtains at the side of the stage. Olive ignores Raymond entirely and continues to stare at the front row as the source of contraband biscuits.

With the official performance over, I hope to sneak the dogs out by the stage door for necessary relief but it becomes instead another chance for some people to meet Olive and Mabel at closer quarters. Photos are requested and although I am occasionally required, I am more often the equivalent of an uncle edging into shot before the official photographer insists, 'Just the bride and groom for this one, thanks.'

For they are the stars. Yes, they are most assuredly just a couple of dogs – but two dogs who have nevertheless made a bit of a difference in recent months and tonight they have delivered well in entertaining us again. As, I imagine, all dogs do every single night, wherever their stage might be.

Wednesday 8 September

From the moment the Olive and Mabel thing really started to become a little bit more than a thing, there was a chance that the twin strands of sport and dogs would eventually tangle up in reality, rather than me providing mock sports commentary while filming them on my phone. And so it has come to pass today.

All of us are at the PGA Championship at Wentworth. The same tournament which took place last October, when we provided coverage from elsewhere and were preoccupied with then making it to a photoshoot. So again, the fact that we are now here on a very hot day in the last dying flare of summer – that crowds are here in their thousands and that it all feels more normal – demonstrates that we are somehow stumbling in a generally forward direction.

Normal again being a relative term, as I have never been asked to bring Olive and Mabel along to a sporting event. Yet here they are – both proudly wearing the official accreditation which they have been given. Mabel takes the common misspelling of her name with good grace and both dogs are delighted to have been granted Access All Areas clearance. Olive uses this enormous privilege to lick the ground close to some wheelie bins.

Their more official duties are unclear. It is really just an opportunity for them to make an appearance on one of the more relaxed days before the tournament proper begins and it does at least prevent the eternal question which I field these days – 'Where are those dogs of yours?' – as I wander round, flanked by two very obvious dogs.

They take part in a charity putting contest, or at least watch and manage to get themselves in the way as the celebrity competitors, Brian McFadden and Keith

Duffy, send shots towards us from a full hundred feet away and, on the deciding putt, the ball of McFadden is stopped on its perfect line no more than a couple of feet from the hole by a small blonde paw, as Mabel was staring up at me at the time awaiting further instruction.

I then take them on to the first tee where they meet with a very warm reception from some and distinctly baffled looks from others – those into whose lives they have not previously trotted. They go on to meet a variety of famous golfers and a few more celebrities who are playing in the Pro-Am, but to Olive and Mabel all are simply other humans and, with the great fairness and levelling eye of dogs, everybody is treated in the same way – judged not upon fame or social standing but only by whether that human might be eating a sandwich at the time.

Finally they head out on to the course with strict instructions that any balls to be found here are strictly off-limits, while also being kept on short leads and in harnesses for fear of the excitement all getting too much for Mabel, inspiring her to one of her mad moments where she might go on an Oscar-style rampage across the greens. There is no chance of such an act from Olive as the heat has reduced her to no more than a black, melted puddle of dog. So Caroline takes them away – untangling leads and those strands of my life, to leave me to get on with my other, very different kind of work. Although just before they leave, I do take time to point out my erstwhile travelling companion, Beef, walking down the fairway and the dogs realise, to their very great disappointment, that they have misunderstood.

Monday 13 September

Today, as has been the case quite often recently, I find myself thinking about dogs a little bit too much. Admittedly I'm doing it with all aspects of life – analysing, dissecting, trying to understand, when it would be far better to keep moving along and not examine every single thing. You don't always have to know how a green screen works – just enjoy the show.

But, the season has changed, the weather now cool and damp with conditions fertile for contemplation and, as I have said, given time to ponder we have the capacity to scratch our heads until they hurt. And since dogs are an ever-present and, almost daily, I am being invited to further expound on the subject, I do find myself musing on their purpose. What more specific description should that accreditation have given? Because observed from a detached viewpoint and neutral eye, their role in life could appear odd.

If members of an alien race should drop in on our planet – merely passing through and using it as some sort of service station, an interstellar Watford Gap on the way somewhere more desirable – I wonder what they would see. Apart from taking a cursory look around and very swiftly deciding that we are making a bit of a bollocks of it all, they may be intrigued by the manner in which we live and many questions would follow, as much of what we humans do appears, at first glance, to make little sense.

Why are these people running when nothing pursues them?

Why does he use so much effort on a machine that goes nowhere?

Why does she constantly stare at this box of lights?

Why do you all argue so much?

More than any of that, they might be fascinated by the different creatures which so many of us have in almost constant attendance. And I would do my very best to clear things up, since a snap social media election has been carried out and I have been delegated pet-explainer-in-chief, while Joe Wicks takes care of the exercise stuff and Justin Bieber has been asked to spell out the rationale behind war.

So, I will ask the head of the alien delegation to walk with me awhile, as he/she/it sends all manner of questions my way:

What is point of this smaller lifeform?

Why is it so constantly pleased?

Why does it clean itself in noisy and public fashion?

And I would try to explain, even if we sometimes can't quite put a finger on it ourselves. This does not relate to working dogs, as their roles are very clear, but to all those others, who trail around after us, just being dogs.

I would perhaps theorise that to see the purpose of a dog you have to also see our human lives – the complicated situations, the tangle of emotions and troubles. See our greater intelligence that is a blessing and a curse to make us capable of both wonderful and hideous things. I would explain that a dog is there as a contrast to all of that – as a counter to all our complexities.

I would go on to say that they teach us so much without being at all aware of the lessons they are passing on. That it is so much better to think of life in simple terms – that it is enough to be warm and fed and safe. Of course we can't live entirely in the simple ways of dogs because we have responsibilities – sleeping ninety per cent of the day and spending the rest of it chasing a ball, digging holes in the garden or staring at a bee would have friends and colleagues concerned – but there is certainly a guidance to be found in their more basic, stripped-back lives. And perhaps most importantly we are constantly shown the love of a dog, which is love at its most fundamental. It is love without a side; it is love that has no unwelcome detail or condition. It is one without jealousy or fear of loss. And I would point out how very much we all need that.

I might draw attention to our own dogs as examples. See how sometimes Mabel looks up at me, as I stroke her chin, with such love and trust that I want to weep. That she can lose herself entirely in her own happy idiocy or that she can race towards you, head down and ears back, as if reaching you is the most important thing in the world – which in her world it is. While Olive stares quietly, thoughtfully – plotting in her dedication to food, but with enough room to be quite fond of her people as well. And besides, her delight when she sees us returning from anywhere at any time tells us the truth and infects us with the same kind of joy at the reunion.

And I might say that for all these reasons I would struggle to be without them. Which rather scares me, because my human love does come with that fear of loss.

So I would close by suggesting that perhaps the purpose of a dog is merely to be a part of our world that offers a glimpse of something else – something untainted by all the unnecessary and unwanted layers which we have added. It is enough that they are simply there, as a comfort and stability. As an escape from us.

All of this I would carefully explain to the alien, who I turn round to find has gone – long since disappeared in search of coffee and a packet of crisps for the onward journey. And for the next few light years at least they would discuss what they had found there on Earth – still wondering about its predominant, but not necessarily preferable, species and more admiring of those others who help us along the way. But all in firm agreement that they still weren't sure what Raymond was.

EPILOGUE

Wednesday 22 September

I write this on a brief pause at home between further stage appearances on our theatre tour, which continues to earn rave reviews. By which I mean it has not yet led to anybody demanding their money back, nor involved Mabel toppling off the stage in the middle of one of her robust but slightly unbalanced scratches.

I'm also preparing for more sports broadcasting, soon to commentate on the Ryder Cup in Wisconsin while not anywhere near Wisconsin and thereafter the London Marathon which we will do in our usual place by Buckingham Palace and the finish line on the Mall. Some things are back to normal. Others may take some time.

Even a few dates into the theatre tour, it all still feels rather absurd, but it has been fun as well. And while the world has plenty enough of the absurd, there is nothing wrong with more of that if it is the variety of oddness that comes cloaked in enjoyment. Since our opener in Bury we have continued to travel up and down the land, dogs asleep in the back as if resting or playing cards in their tour bus, falling into a well-practised routine in Bath and Edinburgh and Buxton, and everywhere the reaction has been the same when the dogs come skipping out of the wings and into reality for the audience.

This has been the positive side of a communal experience – a gathering of hundreds of people who are not clamouring at the gates, or online, or at the abandoned headquarters of a broadcaster, to gripe about any aspect of life which you care to mention. Just people who would like to meet a couple of dogs and their assistant who might have made them laugh in sometimes laughter-free days.

So we have watched some of the Olive and Mabel videos together and talked about how there may or may not be more in the future, because even if I don't have a firm list of plans and plotlines, dogs will inevitably do something to amuse us and I could well be there to film it. But, as I have said before, they certainly can't continue for ever with me wheeling out an increasingly grey-muzzled Olive for the sake of entertainment or circumventing that issue by investing in a digitised, youthful avatar. As for Mabel, well I can see no signs of growing more mature or ageing in the slightest there.

And in one particular way neither of them will age. Whether there is new material or not, I am glad there are already permanent, if somewhat strange, records of them – that these dogs have left some paw prints on the world. Many years from now – if the internet still exists and hasn't risen up to devour us all, funded by embezzlement of our own cryptocurrency – people might stumble across an Olive and Mabel video and enjoy their nonsense. The videos might also be a surreal but quite accurate record of a time when life *has* often been surreal.

I am also glad that they will add to my own memories of them in distant days to come, even as I tell our third or fourth generation of dogs about their illustrious forebears and remind them that they have a great deal to live up to. But at the same time I am sure there will be some sadness that although I can still see Olive and Mabel, I cannot talk to them or touch them. They will be in that undiscovered country – the most unreachable of all those places we are unable to visit. I will see them only in light and glass.

Best then to close the laptop now, while they are here with me. While I can stroke their ears and scratch their backs – while I can feel their warmth and listen to them snoring. While I can talk to them and they can hear me and either tap their tails in recognition at one of the people whom they love, or choose to ignore me as they sleep on, dreaming of squirrels or a low-tabled buffet.

Besides, you have to know when it's time to exit the stage. Illusion, like an intoxication, can lure you towards its charms and the escape which it promises, but life and the world out there still offers far more than that which we have recorded or we see played out on a screen – those limitless but artificial worlds which we create. The real version is certainly far more complicated. No doubt greater in sadness, but also richer in joy. More daunting and fearful, but far more rewarding to the senses. I'm sure that we will continue to tie ourselves up in a confusion of our own making, but as long as there are accompanying creatures to remind us of honesty and simple needs – embodiments of love and trust and optimism, with only occasional bouts of anxiety and neediness – then together we'll be fine.

So I call Olive and Mabel – one who slides half reluctantly and in stages down from the sofa, the other who springs up from her bed and both who shake and stretch to prepare themselves, then trot over at the prospect of release and exploration. We could even look in the depths of the garden for that old orange rubber bone from back at that time when everything started to change. Or perhaps accept that it is gone.

But throughout all that has happened since, these two dogs have been the constants – wanting only small things and always giving so much in return. And pushing at my heels now as I open the door and we step outside together, to see what might be there.

Thank You

To all at Black & White Publishing for their ongoing wisdom, organisation and gentle prodding when required.

To Caroline for all your support and encouragement, for tolerance of numerous dog video productions and for sharing the near-impossible task of trying to dry Mabel.

To Tony Mabey and Iain Cameron, for dog cinematography and photography.

To all who have enjoyed watching, reading about and sharing their own love for these two dogs.

And, of course, to Olive and Mabel themselves, for sometimes agreeing to the usual commands of sit, stay and wait, but also the additional requests of, *'That was good. But can we do it one more time from the top?'* You can't read this, so it's largely pointless, but it's really for other people to see. You are the very best dogs we could ever have hoped for.